DAN SATER

LUXURY
HOME PLANS

Over 100
VIEW-ORIENTED
ESTATE HOMES

PHOTOGRAPH BY: TOM HARPER

A DESIGNS DIRECT PUBLISHING BOOK

Presented by

The Sater Design Collection, Inc.
THE CENTER AT THE SPRINGS
25241 Elementary Way, Suite 201
Bonita Springs, FL 34135

Dan F. Sater, II — CEO and Author

Rickard Bailey — Editor-in-Chief

Jennifer Emmons — Editor

Matt McGarry — Contributing Editor

Clare Ulik — Contributing Editor

Dave Jenkins — Illustrator

Holzhauer — Contributing Illustrator

Diane J. Zwack — Art Director

Kim Campeau — Graphic Artist

Emily Sessa — Graphic Artist

CONTRIBUTING PHOTOGRAPHERS

Everett & Soulé, Tom Harper, Dan Forer, Joseph Lapeyra, Michael Lowry,

William Minarich, Kim Sargent, Bruce Schaeffer, Laurence Taylor,

Doug Thompson, Oscar Thompson and CJ Walker

Front Cover Photo: Dan Forer
Back Cover Photos: Michael Lowry, Laurence Taylor
Front Flap Photo: CJ Walker

Printed by: Toppan Printing Co., Hong Kong

Third Printing: April 2006

10 9 8 7 6 5 4 3

Contents

PHOTOGRAPH BY: LAURENCE TAYLOR

A Work of Art

Throughout the ages, more so than sculpture or painting, architectural design has proven itself the purest form of expression, because it reflects not just the thinking of an age, but its daily living as well. The unique challenge of architecture is not simply to blend artistry and craftsmanship, but to bring these qualities together with a sense of purpose.

Every home, then, is a unique expression of artistry, craftsmanship and purpose. To attribute architectural design to "craftsmanship" does it a disservice. The craftsman, using the tools and materials available to him, attempts only what he knows is possible. It is the artist who is constantly driven to attempt the impossible, or at least the improbable. Without artistry, a design is uninspired, and without purpose, it has no reason for being, no function.

In the following pages, you'll discover over 100 home designs where the aim is to blend artistry and function. Graceful arches and stoic columns, ornate balustrades and stately turrets, grand entries and vast interior spaces — each of these homes is rich in architectural heritage. Yet, these homes were designed to be purposeful as well as beautiful. Flowing floor plans create infinitely livable family space. Expanses of glass and retreating glass walls welcome the exterior landscape into the interior. Ergonomic gourmet kitchens are as functional as they are fashionable.

As we set out to design a true luxury home, we at Sater Design Collection attempt to meet all of the needs of the modern family. We create spaces for dining, sleeping, studying and entertaining. But, we also try to create spaces that motivate, uplift and satisfy in the profoundest sense. We consider our work as art and our inspiration the American family.

We define luxury not as opulence, but as vibrancy. The strength of detail and character in our designs, we trust, reflect this philosophy.

I hope you will be inspired and motivated by these designs, and that among these pages, you will find the perfect place to call home.

God bless,

Dan F. Sater II, AIBD

PLAN | *6910a Fiorentino*

Photography: Dan Forer

PHOTO ABOVE: *The design touches of Andrea Palladio, one of the great architects of the sixteenth century, can be seen in this aristocratic country residence, a villa that could have been transported from a hillside in northern Italy. The softness of the low-pitch roofs, in juxtaposition to the magnificent rotunda that dominates the front elevation, gives this villa's entrance an aura of serene elegance.*

PHOTO RIGHT: *Despite its spacious 600 square feet, the leisure room is still one of the coziest rooms in the home, featuring a corner fireplace, built-in entertainment center, exposed-beam ceiling and zero-corner sliding glass doors that open onto the loggia.*

PHOTO FAR RIGHT: *With its soaring, twenty-foot vaulted ceiling, towering Ionic columns and graceful arches, this superbly spacious rotunda living area is, without a doubt, the heart and soul of the home.*

PHOTO ABOVE: *A breezy, rambling loggia wraps the rear elevation. Decorative columns and pillars gracefully bear a beautiful burden — the weight of a second-story observation deck that opens into the starry sky above.*

PHOTO RIGHT: *The master suite is truly a haven, replete with morning kitchen and his-and-her walk-in closets. One of the crown jewels in this opulent design, the sitting area opens to the loggia via French doors. For pure enjoyment, simply add an evening cocktail or morning coffee.*

PHOTO FAR RIGHT: *Rich accents in wood bring an aura of Old World grace and sophistication to a private study adjacent to the formal living room.*

PHOTO RIGHT: *This Italianate-style rotunda staircase, with its sleek balustrade, vertical windows, mile-high exposed-beam ceiling and smooth curves and arches, appears to break the bonds of earth and disappear into the heavens.*

PHOTO BELOW: *Retreating glass doors create a seamless transition between the leisure room and the loggia's outdoor kitchen, enabling the chef of the home to grill steaks and watch a favorite sporting event at the same time.*

PHOTO ABOVE: *The loft above the dining area— its boundaries defined by an ornate, wrought-iron railing — provides access to two spacious, second-story guest suites and an observation deck, not to mention a picturesque view of the beautifully appointed first floor.*

PHOTO ABOVE: *The emphasis might appear to be more on "form" than "function," but don't be deceived — this picture-perfect kitchen is deceptively hard-working. Enjoying ample space for a professional-grade hooded range, double sinks and spacious dual pantries, the chef of this home could easily manage a dinner party for twelve.*

PHOTO RIGHT: *An elevated garden tub in the master suite overlooks the privacy garden. Three vertical arched windows, virtually floor to ceiling, bring both elegance and illumination to the scene, without compromising privacy.*

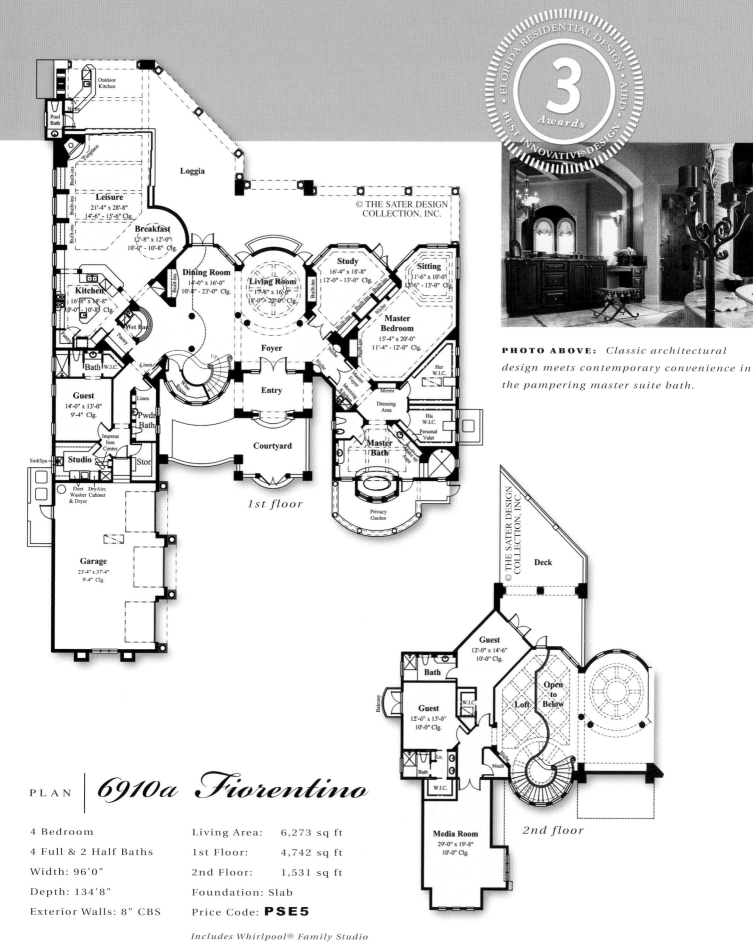

Outdoor Kitchen

Pool Bath

Niche

Fireplace

Loggia

Leisure
21'-4" x 28'-8"
14'-6" - 15'-6" Clg.

Built-ins

Breakfast
12'-8" x 12'-0"
10'-0" - 10'-8" Clg.

Dining Room
14'-0" x 16'-0"
10'-8" - 23'-0" Clg.

Living Room
17'-8" x 16'-0"
18'-0" - 20'-0" Clg.

Study
16'-4" x 18'-8"
12'-0" - 13'-0" Clg.

Sitting
11'-6" x 10'-0"
13'-6" - 13'-0" Clg.

© THE SATER DESIGN
COLLECTION, INC.

Kitchen
16'-8" x 18'-8"
10'-0" - 10'-8"

Wet Bar

Pantry

Master Bedroom
15'-4" x 20'-0"
11'-4" - 12'-0" Clg.

Foyer

Niche

Wine Room

Bath   W.I.C.

Linen

Guest
14'-0" x 13'-0"
9'-4" Clg.

Linen

Pwdr Bath

Entry

Master Foyer

Morning Kitchen

Her W.I.C.

Mirror

Dressing Area

His W.I.C.

Personal Valet

Impress Iron Center

Stor

Courtyard

Make-up Area

Master Bath

SinkSpa

Studio

Duet DryAire Washer Cabinet & Dryer

Privacy Garden

1st floor

Garage
23'-4" x 37'-4"
9'-4" Clg.

© THE SATER DESIGN COLLECTION, INC.

Deck

Guest
12'-0" x 14'-6"
10'-0" Clg.

Bath

Balcony

Guest
12'-0" x 13'-0"
10'-0" Clg.

W.I.C.

Loft

Open to Below

Niche

Mech

Bath

Ln.

W.I.C.

Media Room
29'-0" x 19'-8"
10'-0" Clg.

2nd floor

PLAN | *6910a Fiorentino*

4 Bedroom

4 Full & 2 Half Baths

Width: 96'0"

Depth: 134'8"

Exterior Walls: 8" CBS

Living Area: 6,273 sq ft

1st Floor: 4,742 sq ft

2nd Floor: 1,531 sq ft

Foundation: Slab

Price Code: **PSE5**

Includes Whirlpool® Family Studio

Please note: Home photographed may differ from blueprint.

Photography: Michael Lowry

PHOTO ABOVE: *True to its Spanish Revival heritage — low-pitched hipped roofs, an elaborate carved entry, red barrel tile and a stately cupola — this spectacular estate home is an eight-thousand-square-foot work of art. It is no surprise that this design garnered a first-place award in the Parade of Homes competition.*

PHOTO RIGHT: *The very definition of a "room with a view," the Grand Solana demonstrates beautifully this layout's love affair with the great outdoors and scenic opportunities it presents.*

PHOTO FAR RIGHT: *The formal dining room — with its barrel-vault ceiling, carved coffers and Corinthian columns — displays an almost surreal beauty — the kind one sees more often in a still-life painting than a photograph.*

TOP PHOTO: *Reminiscent of the tiered arches and Tuscan columns of Rome's Colosseum and the majestic country villas of Rome's noble families, this spectacular Solana is a classic example of ageless, architectural beauty.*

BOTTOM LEFT: *The notion that a home must "live" in harmony with the outside world was a concept held in high regard by Roman architects, and is beautifully articulated here in this luxurious lanai.*

BOTTOM RIGHT: *On either end of the breakfast bar, decorative columns support a stepped ceiling and, at the same time, create two graceful arches that define the kitchen entry.*

PHOTO LEFT: *Decorative pillars and columns demonstrate the influence of the ancient Greeks in this magnificent master bath, while a luxurious whirpool tub offers a very modern convenience.*

PHOTO ABOVE: *Sequestered in a far corner of the floor plan, this opulent master suite with sitting room provides the seclusion and tranquility that is absolutely essential at the end of a busy day.*

PHOTO ABOVE: *A massive, ornately carved hearth both anchors and warms the Grand Solana and the majestic foyer adjacent. Corinthian columns support soaring volume ceilings like gods of mythology bearing the weight of the heavens.*

PHOTO RIGHT: *At night, architectural lighting highlights the home's decorative corbels and columns, adding even more drama to an already dramatic rear elevation.*

© THE SATER DESIGN COLLECTION, INC.

1st floor

PHOTO ABOVE: *Double doors in the master suite open onto a very private lanai.*

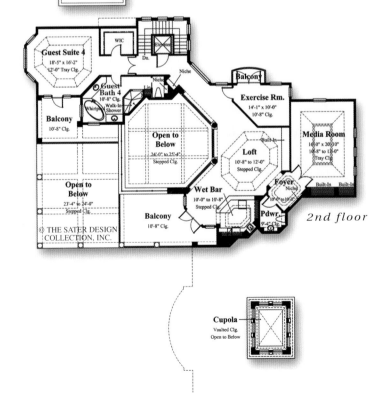

PHOTO ABOVE: *The loft, with wet bar, serves as a fabulous game or billiard room.*

© THE SATER DESIGN COLLECTION, INC.

2nd floor

Cupola
Vaulted Clg.
Open to Below

PLAN | *6940* *Alamosa*

5 Bedroom

5 Full & 2 Half Baths

Width: 118'0"

Depth: 147'10"

Exterior Walls: 8" CBS

Living Area: 8,088 sq ft

1st Floor: 6,122 sq ft

2nd Floor: 1,966 sq ft

Foundation: Slab

Price Code: **PSE5**

Please note: Home photographed may differ from blueprint.

Photography: Tom Harper

PHOTO ABOVE: *Sculpted masonry, circle-head windows, shapely pilasters and a graceful arched entry create a majestic façade for this picturesque, Mediterranean Revival-style seaside villa. The interior of this seven-thousand-square-foot estate is both beautiful and functional, blending classical architectural design with the demands and desires of 21st-century living.*

PHOTO RIGHT: *A taste for spectacular views? Crowned by a round coffer, this circular dining room's one-hundred-eighty degrees of glass serves up incredible vistas of the exterior landscape.*

PHOTO ABOVE: *One could easily imagine a grove of olive trees just beyond the expansive windows of this Mediterranean-style living room. On a cool evening, the room is warmed by an ornate fireplace with mantel supported by rusticated pillars.*

PHOTO LEFT: *Reminiscent of the magnificent architecture of Italian cathedrals, graceful arches and columns give the entry a "serene grandness."*

TOP PHOTO: *A sprawling wraparound lanai and multiple decks on both the first and second story, as well as a privacy garden off the master bath, make the exterior landscape readily accessible.*

BOTTOM LEFT: *The leisure room is well equipped for rest and relaxation, with fireplace and retreating glass doors that open to the lanai.*

BOTTOM CENTER & RIGHT: *Behind the bar, accessible from the kitchen, is a spectacular 1,700-bottle wine cellar — the perfect home for that 1954 magnum of Dom Perignon.*

PHOTO ABOVE: *Two sensibilities meet in this master bath: those of the ancient Greeks in classic design and those of modern man in a love of modern conveniences.*

PHOTO LEFT: *This gourmet kitchen satisfies even the most voracious appetite for culinary accoutrements. Generous cabinet and pantry space are everywhere, as well as state-of-the-art built-in appliances.*

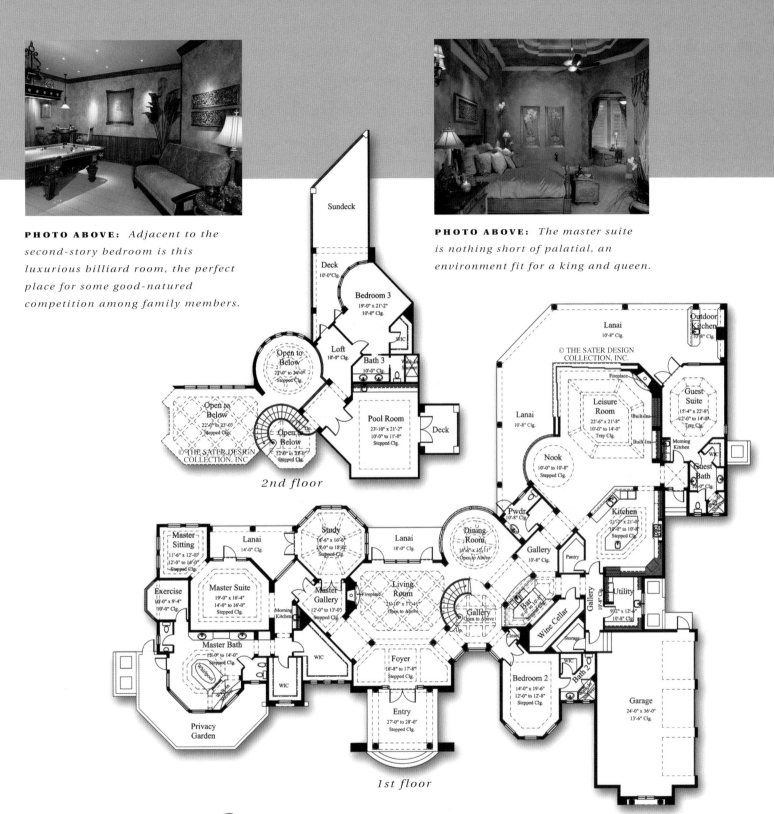

PHOTO ABOVE: *Adjacent to the second-story bedroom is this luxurious billiard room, the perfect place for some good-natured competition among family members.*

PHOTO ABOVE: *The master suite is nothing short of palatial, an environment fit for a king and queen.*

Sundeck

Deck
10'-0" Clg.

Bedroom 3
19'-0" x 21'-2"
10'-0" Clg.

Open to Below
22'-0" to 24'-0"
Stepped Clg.

Loft
10'-0" Clg.

Bath 3
10'-0" Clg.

WIC

Open to Below
22'-0" to 33'-0"
Stepped Clg.

Open to Below
22'-0" to 24'-0"
Stepped Clg.

© THE SATER DESIGN COLLECTION, INC

Pool Room
23'-10" x 21'-2"
10'-0" to 11'-0"
Stepped Clg.

Deck

2nd floor

Lanai
10'-8" Clg.

Outdoor Kitchen
10'-8" Clg.

© THE SATER DESIGN COLLECTION, INC.

Lanai
10'-8" Clg.

Leisure Room
22'-6" x 21'-8"
10'-0" to 14'-0"
Tray Clg.

Guest Suite
15'-4" x 22'-8"
12'-0" to 14'-0"
Tray Clg.

Fireplace

Built-Ins

Built-Ins

Morning Kitchen

Nook
10'-0" to 10'-8"
Stepped Clg.

Guest Bath
10'-0" Clg.

WIC

Pwdr.
10'-8" Clg.

Kitchen
21'-2" x 21'-0"
10'-0" to 10'-8"
Stepped Clg.

Master Sitting
11'-6" x 12'-0"
12'-0" to 14'-0"
Stepped Clg.

Lanai
14'-0" Clg.

Study
16'-6" x 16'-6"
9'-0" to 18'-0"
Stepped Clg.

Lanai
18'-0" Clg.

Dining Room
16'-4" x 15'-1"
Open to Above

Gallery
10'-8" Clg.

Pantry

Exercise
10'-0" x 9'-4"
10'-0" Clg.

Master Suite
19'-0" x 16'-4"
14'-0" to 16'-0"
Stepped Clg.

Morning Kitchen

Master Gallery
12'-0" x 13'-0"
Stepped Clg.

Fireplace

Living Room
21'-2" x 21'-4"
Open to Above

Gallery
Open to Above

Bar
9'-2" x 10'-8"

Wine Cellar

Gallery
10'-8" Clg.

Utility
9'-2" x 12'-4"
10'-8" Clg.

Master Bath
23'-0" x 14'-0"
Stepped Clg.

Whirlpool

Walk-In Shower

Master Bath
10'-0" Clg.

WIC

WIC

Closet

Storage

Foyer
16'-8" x 17'-8"
Stepped Clg.

Bedroom 2
14'-0" x 19'-6"
12'-0" to 12'-8"
Stepped Clg.

WIC

Bath 2

Garage
24'-0" x 36'-0"
13'-6" Clg.

Privacy Garden

Entry
27'-0" to 28'-0"
Stepped Clg.

1st floor

PLAN | *6937* *Trissino*

4 Bedroom

4-1/2 Bath

Width: 142'7"

Depth: 118'0"

Exterior Walls: 8" CBS

Living Area: 7,209 sq ft

1st Floor: 6,134 sq ft

2nd Floor: 1,075 sq ft

Foundation: Slab

Price Code: **PSE5**

PHOTO LEFT PAGE: *The vaulted living room draws natural light — not to mention scenic views — from a wall of glass and a pair of classic French doors, while a sleek staircase wends its way to a second-story loft.*

Please note: Home photographed may differ from blueprint. Not available for construction in Lee or Collier Counties, Florida.

PLAN | *6753a Autumn Woods*

Photography: Laurence Taylor

PHOTO ABOVE: *Winner of a first-place award from the American Institute of Building Design, this Mediterranean manor glitters like a precious gem beneath the twilight sky. And like any rare stone, there is no other like it.*

PHOTO RIGHT: *A Renaissance Revival-style entry, recognizable by columns supporting the arched opening, creates a grand entrance.*

PHOTO ABOVE: Bay windows offer diners a panoramic view, while decorative columns stand close by, setting the boundaries between foyer and dining area.

PHOTO RIGHT: Dark corners are a rare commodity indeed in the octagonal study, thanks to its soaring vaulted ceiling and an array of bay windows.

PHOTO ABOVE: *Panoramic floor-to-ceiling windows in the breakfast nook bring a magnificent sunrise view with each morning cup of coffee.*

TOP PHOTO: *Casual and cozy, this corner-pocket living room offers visitors a warm welcome, courtesy of its beautifully crafted, tile fireplace and angled view.*

PHOTO ABOVE: *In the Old World tradition, the kitchen is both friendly and intimate, making it as much a place for casual conversation as for cooking.*

PLAN | *6753a Autumn Woods*

PHOTO ABOVE: *A Mediterranean-style fireplace, tucked in a cozy corner of the lanai, brings warmth to any outdoor gathering.*

PHOTO LEFT: *Ochre-colored stucco, terracotta tile, turquoise pool and azure sky work in concert — creating an image that one might see on a postcard from an Aegean Sea resort.*

PHOTO ABOVE: *A bath with a view! The master suite allows the owners of the house an opportunity to luxuriate in a warm bath while enjoying views of the garden.*

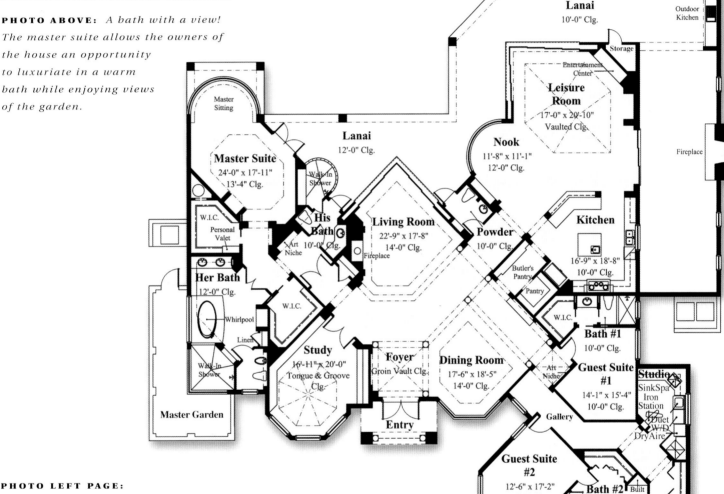

PHOTO LEFT PAGE:

The diamond-shaped leisure room is conveniently located adjacent to the kitchen, which means that snacks are just a few steps away.

PLAN | *6753a Autumn Woods*

3 Bedroom

4-1/2 Bath

Width: 87'2"

Depth: 127'11"

Exterior Walls: 8" CBS

Living Area: 4,534 sq ft

Foundation: Slab

Price Code: **PSE5**

Includes Whirlpool® Family Studio

Please note: Home photographed may differ from blueprint.

Photography: Tom Harper

PHOTO ABOVE: *In the flowing, festive style of a Mediterranean manor, this majestic villa would make a "grand entrance" in even the most exclusive neighborhoods. The defining characteristic of its façade is a stately pair of turrets, standing somewhat stoic and taciturn behind a grand carved and open entry, "upstaged" by a pair of decorative columns. Just beyond, a magnificent set of carved double doors beckons.*

PHOTO RIGHT: *French doors lead from the foyer to a cozy, octagonal-shaped retreat — a restful study. Imagine a comfortable chair at the end of a busy day, the sun's last rays streaming through three Palladian-style windows.*

PHOTO ABOVE: *Two elegant rooms in which to relax become one when the leisure room's corner sliding glass doors are pushed aside, making room for a sprawling covered lanai with outdoor kitchen. The lanai features a charming banco-style fireplace that creates a warm gathering place for family and friends.*

PHOTO LEFT: *A trio of floor-to-ceiling windows opens onto the covered lanai. Only these well-placed windows separate the living room from the scenic landscape beyond.*

PHOTO ABOVE: *The gourmet kitchen is more a work of art and a culinary masterpiece, perhaps, than a place for preparing meals, although it is certainly well equipped for just that, with its hooded range, double ovens and roomy walk-in pantry.*

PHOTO RIGHT: *The glass-enclosed rooms of the rear elevation defy the label "interior" space. From one side of the home to the other, the outside is welcomed in via expansive glass windows and retreating glass doors.*

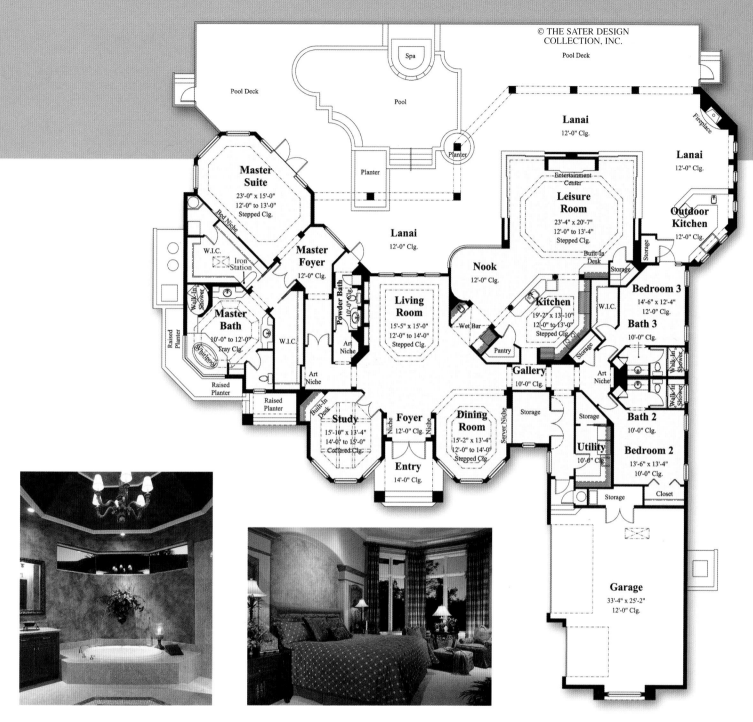

© THE SATER DESIGN COLLECTION, INC.

Pool Deck

Spa

Pool

Pool Deck

Lanai
12'-0" Clg.

Lanai
12'-0" Clg.

Master Suite
23'-0" x 15'-0"
12'-0" to 13'-0"
Stepped Clg.

Bed Niche

Fireplace

Leisure Room
23'-4" x 20'-7"
12'-0" to 13'-4"
Stepped Clg.

Entertainment Center

Outdoor Kitchen
12'-0" Clg.

W.I.C.

Iron Station

Master Foyer
12'-0" Clg.

Lanai
12'-0" Clg.

Nook
12'-0" Clg.

Built-In Desk

Storage

Storage

Bedroom 3
14'-6" x 12'-4"
12'-0" Clg.

Walk-In Shower

Master Bath
10'-0" to 12'-0"

Powder Bath
10'-0" Clg.

Living Room
15'-5" x 15'-0"
12'-0" to 14'-0"
Stepped Clg.

Kitchen
19'-2" x 13'-10"
12'-0" to 13'-0"
Stepped Clg.

Wet Bar

W.I.C.

Bath 3
10'-0" Clg.

Raised Planter

Whirlpool

Tray Clg.

W.I.C.

Art Niche

Pantry

Storage

Gallery
10'-0" Clg.

Art Niche

Walk-In Shower

Raised Planter

Art Niche

Raised Planter

Built-In Desk

Study
15'-10" x 13'-4"
14'-0" to 15'-0"
Coffered Clg.

Niche

Foyer
12'-0" Clg.

Niche

Dining Room
15'-2" x 13'-4"
12'-0" to 14'-0"
Stepped Clg.

Server Niche

Storage

Storage

Utility
10'-0" Clg.

Bath 2
10'-0" Clg.

Walk-In Shower

Bedroom 2
13'-6" x 13'-4"
10'-0" Clg.

Entry
14'-0" Clg.

Storage

Closet

Garage
33'-4" x 25'-2"
12'-0" Clg.

PHOTO ABOVE: *The Italianate-style master bath boasts a magnificent whirpool garden tub. (Bubble bath not included.)*

PHOTO ABOVE: *The theme of graceful arches flows into the master suite, as evidenced here by the arch-top bed niche.*

PLAN | *6936 McKiney*

3 Bedroom

3-1/2 Bath

Width: 104'0"

Depth: 111'0"

Exterior Walls: 8" CBS

Living Area: 4,302 sq ft

Foundation: Slab

Price Code: **PSE5**

Please note: Home photographed may differ from blueprint.

PLAN | *6934* *Avondale*

Photography: Tom Harper and Doug Thompson

PHOTO ABOVE: *Winner of three distinguished awards, this majestic British Colonial design boldly blends luxury and livability. Its grand façade, punctuated by dual porte-cocheres, is a mere prelude to what waits within.*

PHOTO RIGHT: *A barrel-vault ceiling in the formal entry and stepped ceiling in the living room, respectively, give this view from the lanai a sense of spacious elegance.*

PHOTO FAR RIGHT: *Picturesque panoramas and wide-open spaces—seen here in the leisure room— are everywhere you turn, courtesy of retreating glass doors and volume ceilings throughout.*

PHOTO ABOVE: *Designed with ergonomics in mind, the gourmet kitchen is comfortable and efficient. A prime example is the butler's pantry, which is conveniently accessible from both the kitchen and the dining room.*

PHOTO RIGHT: *Walls seem to simply disappear as the retreating glass doors of the leisure room (left) and living room (right) are opened onto the lanai.*

PHOTO ABOVE: *With two sets of double doors that open onto a deck, guests always have the option of dining al fresco.*

PHOTO ABOVE: *A soaring arched ceiling, over twenty-feet from the floor at its peak, brings a touch of drama to an otherwise relaxed and informal leisure room.*

PHOTO ABOVE: *This strikingly unique, octagonal master bath features a walk-in shower for two, garden tub and garden views.*

PHOTO ABOVE: *The master suite, with sitting room, is both roomy and intimate. Adjacent is a generous walk-in closet.*

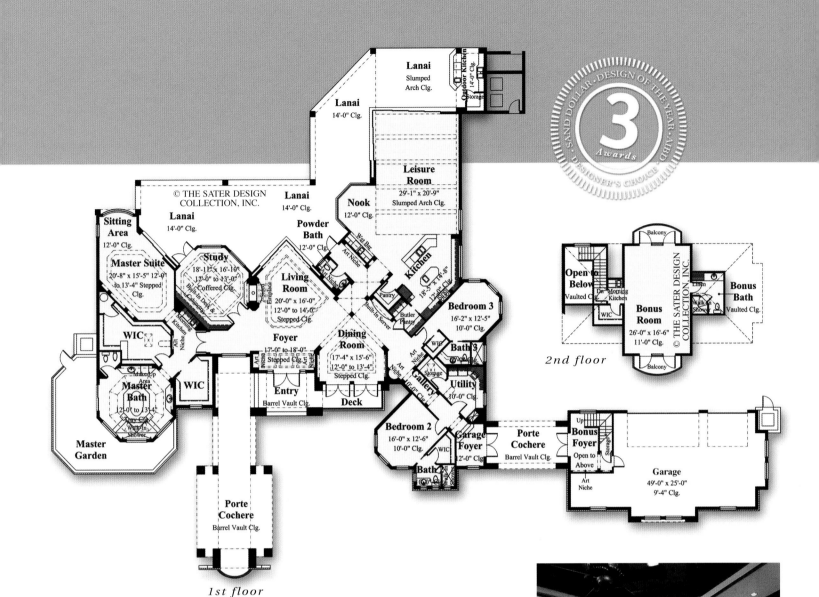

© THE SATER DESIGN
COLLECTION, INC.

Lanai
Slumped
Arch Clg.

Lanai
14'-0" Clg.

Outdoor Kitchen

Storage

Leisure Room
29'-1" x 20'-9"
Slumped Arch Clg.

Lanai
14'-0" Clg.

Nook
12'-0" Clg.

Lanai
14'-0" Clg.

Sitting Area
12'-0" Clg.

Powder Bath
12'-0" Clg.

Kitchen
18'-5" x 14'-8"
12'-0" Clg.

Study
18'-11" x 16'-10"
12'-0" to 13'-0"
Coffered Clg.

Living Room
20'-0" x 16'-0"
12'-0" to 14'-0"
Stepped Clg.

Master Suite
20'-8" x 15'-5" 12'-0"
to 13'-4" Stepped
Clg.

Bedroom 3
16'-2" x 12'-5"
10'-0" Clg.

WIC

Foyer
17'-0" to 18'-0"
Stepped Clg.

Dining Room
17'-4" x 15'-6"
12'-0" to 13'-4"
Stepped Clg.

Gallery

Bath 3

Utility
10'-0" Clg.

WIC

Master Bath
12'-0" to 13'-4"
Tray Clg.
Walk-In Shower

Entry
Barrel Vault Clg.

Deck

Bedroom 2
16'-0" x 12'-6"
10'-0" Clg.

Garage Foyer
12'-0" Clg.

Porte Cochere
Barrel Vault Clg.

Bonus Foyer
Open to Above

Garage
49'-0" x 25'-0"
9'-4" Clg.

Art Niche

Bath

Master Garden

Porte Cochere
Barrel Vault Clg.

1st floor

Open to Below
Vaulted Clg.

Bonus Room
26'-0" x 16'-6"
11'-0" Clg.

Bonus Bath
Vaulted Clg.

Balcony

Balcony

© THE SATER DESIGN COLLECTION, INC.

2nd floor

TOP PHOTO OPPOSITE PAGE:

The formal living room invites scenic vistas through retreating glass doors. To the left, a two-sided fireplace of carved stone warms both this room and the adjacent study.

PLAN | **6934** *Avondale*

3 Bedroom

4-1/2 Bath

Width: 168'9"

Depth: 125'4"

Exterior Walls: 8" CBS

Living Area: 5,612 sq ft

1st Floor: 4,880 sq ft

2nd Floor: 732 sq ft

Foundation: Slab

Price Code: **PSE5**

PHOTO ABOVE: *A favorite novel and a warm fire make the ideal finishing touches to this intimate study.*

Please note: Home photographed may differ from blueprint. Not available for construction in Lee or Collier Counties, Florida.

Photography: Laurence Taylor

PHOTO ABOVE: *Subtly British Colonial, this spectacular design yearns to fix its gaze on ships laden with spices and sugar cane floating on a turquoise sea. Its sun-soaked stucco, modest stone trim work, turrets and gently pitched roofs are hallmarks of this informal "island" architecture. Mitered-glass walls, sliding glass doors and a second-story deck bring the outside in, while a rambling lanai with outdoor kitchen and powder room bring ease and elegance to outdoor entertaining.*

PHOTO RIGHT: *A wet bar, with powder room opposite, tucks neatly into an arched alcove. This series of arches, supported by decorative columns, defines the gallery area linking the leisure room to the dining area.*

PHOTO ABOVE: *Exquisite crown molding gives an aura of sophistication to an otherwise very relaxed living area, while retreating sliding glass doors provide a sweeping view of the patio and landscape beyond.*

PHOTO LEFT: *As if dueling "His" and "Her" baths weren't enough, this semi-circular sitting room off the master suite, with its floor-to-ceiling radius glass, is the perfect place for relaxing — and stargazing.*

PHOTO ABOVE: *Graceful arches unite the living room and dining area. The home's open floor plan, in combination with sky-high ceilings, brings living, dining, foyer and gallery areas together to create a first-floor layout that is both functional and fashionable.*

PHOTOS RIGHT & FAR RIGHT: *The home's gourmet kitchen, roomy enough to easily accommodate "too many chefs," boasts a large walk-in pantry, double ovens and center island with vegetable sink and food-prep area. The "pièce de résistance" of this generous layout is the single-paned window with hood molding that offers a view of the outdoor fireplace just beyond the covered lanai.*

46

PHOTO ABOVE: *A perfect place for relaxing under the stars, the courtyard features an outdoor fireplace of stucco, tile and stone flanked by a pair of grand, rusticated stone columns.*

PHOTO RIGHT: *The rear elevation is distinguished by a covered wraparound lanai, accessible from several rooms in the home including the master suite, living area, leisure room and separate guest suite. In short, outdoor entertaining made easy.*

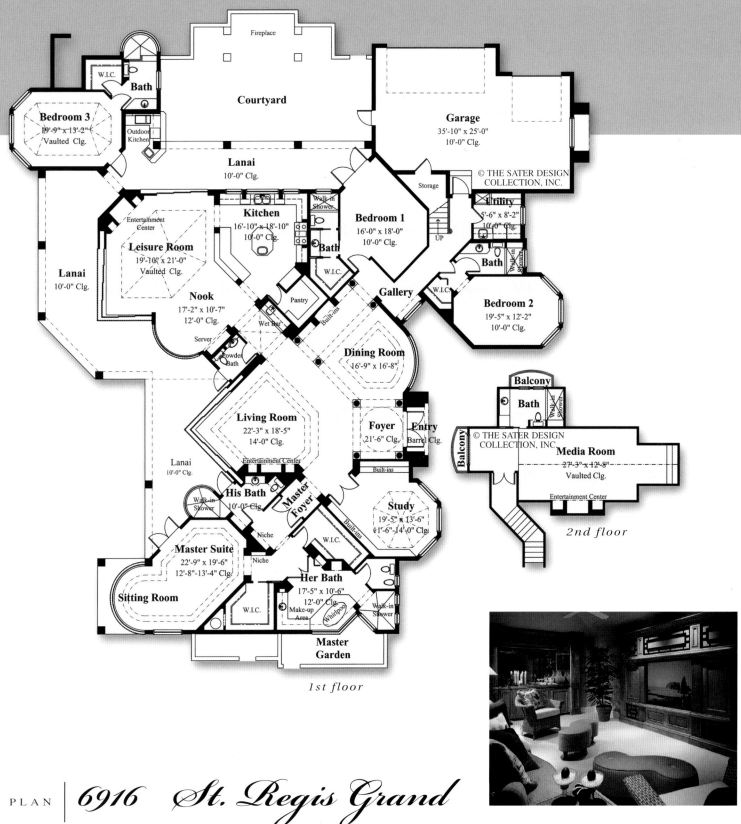

1st floor

2nd floor

PLAN | *6916* *St. Regis Grand*

4 Bedroom

6-1/2 Bath

Width: 106'6"

Depth: 106'0"

Exterior Walls: 8" CBS

Living Area: 5,265 sq ft

1st Floor: 4,784 sq ft

2nd Floor: 481 sq ft

Foundation: Slab

Price Code: **PSE5**

PHOTO ABOVE: *Tucked away in the corner of the home, on the second story, this roomy and relaxing media room makes the perfect escape at the end of a busy day.*

Please note: Home photographed may differ from blueprint.

Photography: Laurence Taylor

PHOTO ABOVE: *Winner of an American Institute of Building Design Award, this stately villa draws inspiration from classical Old World architecture. The defining feature is without a doubt its stunning two-story, Palladian-style rotunda, flanked by a magnificent windowed turret.*

PHOTO RIGHT: *Designed after the Georgian vernacular, exemplified best by Jefferson's Monticello, this highly sculpted façade featuring decorative columns and graceful arches creates a magnificent welcome. At night, the illuminated cupola serves almost as a beacon, giving the front elevation of the home a unique and unmistakable countenance.*

PHOTO ABOVE: *The grand hall transitions seamlessly to the formal salon nestled beneath a second-story balcony. Meanwhile, an elegant radial staircase curves its way to the guest suites above and a sitting loft with balcony.*

PHOTO LEFT: *Twenty-two feet in diameter and supported by tapered columns, the home's spacious grand hall is nothing less than spectacular. Natural light streams in from circular windows—a full thirty-six feet above the floor.*

PHOTO ABOVE: *The master bath has an Old World feel, with free-standing columns, a gorgeous garden tub in the center and a sunken shower that overlooks the master suite's private garden.*

PHOTO RIGHT: *The expansive master suite transitions into an adjoining octagonal sitting room, replete with scenic views and a conveniently located morning kitchen.*

PHOTO FAR RIGHT: *With its floor-to-ceiling arched window, this sunken shower becomes a cascading waterfall hidden in a tropical paradise.*

PHOTO ABOVE: *This gourmet kitchen is "twice as nice," with its dual islands, double ovens and sinks. Above the cooktop, a magnificent portrait-oriented window offers a beautifully framed view of the exterior landscape.*

PHOTO LEFT: *A 180-degree, floor-to-ceiling bay window gives dinner guests a real taste of the great outdoors with a bigger-than-life panoramic view across the veranda.*

PHOTO ABOVE: *The veranda sitting area with fireplace and outdoor kitchen makes a cozy, sheltered spot for a warm drink on cool evenings.*

TOP PHOTO: *One of the home's highlights is its wraparound veranda. Then again, the second-story observation deck, accessible from an octagonal sitting loft, is pretty spectacular as well.*

PHOTO ABOVE: *An open floor plan removes boundaries between living areas and creates functional space galore, as seen here in the view from the kitchen to the leisure room.*

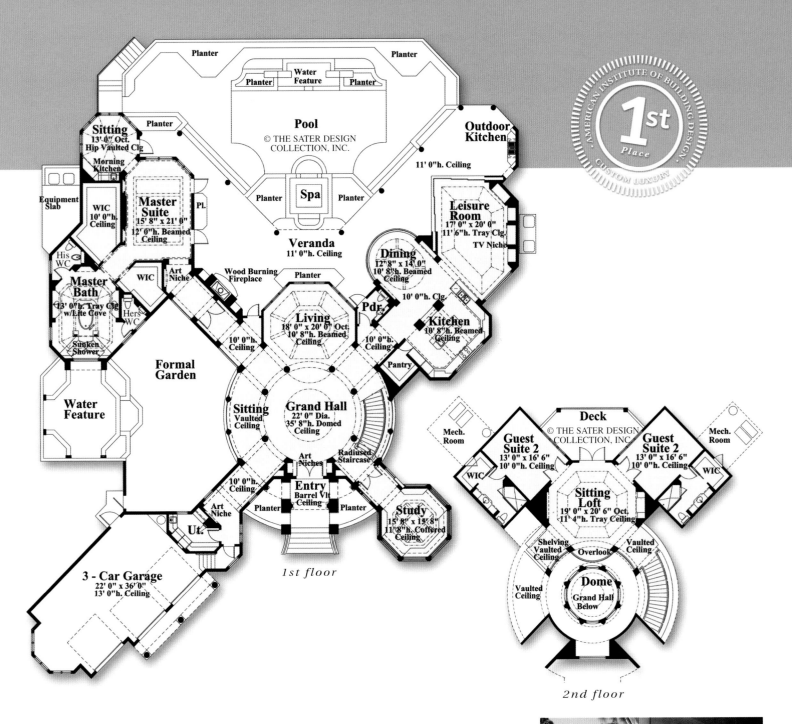

Pool

© THE SATER DESIGN COLLECTION, INC.

Planter — Planter
Water Feature
Planter — Planter

Outdoor Kitchen
11' 0"h. Ceiling

Sitting
13' 0" Oct.
Hip Vaulted Clg

Planter

Morning Kitchen

Equipment Slab

WIC
10' 0"h. Ceiling

Master Suite
15' 8" x 21' 0"
12' 0"h. Beamed Ceiling

Pl.

Leisure Room
17' 0" x 20' 0"
11' 6"h. Tray Clg.

TV Niche

His WC

Master Bath
13' 0"h. Tray Clg w/Lite Cove

Hers WC

WIC

Art Niche

Wood Burning Fireplace

Planter

Dining
12' 8" x 14' 0"
10' 8"h. Beamed Ceiling

10' 0" h. Clg.

Veranda
11' 0"h. Ceiling

Spa

Planter — Planter

Sunken Shower

Formal Garden

Water Feature

Living
18' 0" x 20' 0" Oct.
10' 8"h. Beamed Ceiling

Pdr.

10' 0" h. Ceiling

Kitchen
10' 8"h. Beamed Ceiling

Pantry

10' 0"h. Ceiling

Sitting
Vaulted Ceiling

Grand Hall
22' 0" Dia.
35' 8" Domed Ceiling

Art Niches

Radiused Staircase

10' 0"h. Ceiling

Art Niche

Entry
Barrel Vlt Ceiling

Planter — Planter

Study
15' 8" x 15' 8"
11' 8"h. Coffered Ceiling

Ut.

3 - Car Garage
22' 0" x 36' 0"
13' 0"h. Ceiling

1st floor

Deck

© THE SATER DESIGN COLLECTION, INC

Mech. Room

Guest Suite 2
13' 0" x 16' 6"
10' 0"h. Ceiling

WIC

Mech. Room

Guest Suite 2
13' 0" x 16' 6"
10' 0"h. Ceiling

WIC

Sitting Loft
19' 0" x 20' 6" Oct.
11' 4"h. Tray Ceiling

Shelving Vaulted Ceiling

Overlook

Vaulted Ceiling

Vaulted Ceiling

Dome
Grand Hall Below

2nd floor

PLAN | **6922** *Prestonwood*

3 Bedroom

3-1/2 Bath

Width: 117'2"

Depth: 131'7"

Exterior Walls: 8" CBS

Living Area: 5,924 sq ft

1st Floor: 4,715 sq ft

2nd Floor: 1,209 sq ft

Foundation: Slab

Price Code: **PSE5**

Please note: Home photographed may differ from blueprint.

PHOTO ABOVE: *One could easily imagine the rolling hillside vineyards of Chianti just beyond the home's veranda.*

PLAN | *6672a Monterray Lane*

Photography: Laurence Taylor

PHOTO ABOVE: *Modern sensibility meets Spanish Colonial heritage in this quintessential Mediterranean seaside resort home. In contrast to its casual façade, with its stucco and rambling red-barrel-tile roof, the home's interior exhibits the noble simplicity and calm grandeur of classic Greek architecture.*

PHOTO RIGHT: *Stone columns, like stoic sentries standing guard, flank a Spanish Colonial-style recessed entry.*

PHOTO FAR RIGHT: *Spatial qualities of ancient architecture — the domed and vaulted spaces of ancient Rome in particular — give the formal dining area an almost Cathedral-like quality.*

PHOTO ABOVE: *Well-appointed with double ovens, roomy walk-in pantry and center island, this kitchen beautifully blends function and fashion.*

PHOTO RIGHT: *In the leisure room, built-ins segue seamlessly to retreating glass doors, all under an octagonal vaulted ceiling.*

PHOTO ABOVE: *The ultimate in restful retreats, the living room features corner-pocket sliding glass doors that open onto a windswept lanai. Cool sea breezes are warmed by the fireplace, beautifully crafted of tile and stone.*

PHOTO ABOVE: *The generously sized master's suite — nearly five-hundred-square-feet — affords a magnificent panoramic view of the exterior landscape through a floor-to-ceiling bay window.*

TOP PHOTO: *Drawing on coastal vernaculars, the rear elevation celebrates life in the great outdoors, with its retreating glass doors, wraparound lanai and outdoor kitchen.*

PHOTO ABOVE: *This spacious, yet very private, master bath boasts high stepped ceiling, garden tub, his-and-her vanities and walk-in closets, making it a luxurious space fit for a king and queen.*

© THE SATER DESIGN COLLECTION, INC.

Outdoor Kitchen

Master Suite
18'-10" x 19'-11"
11'-0" to 13'-0"
Stepped Clg.
— bed art niche

Sitting Area

Walk-in Shower

Leisure Room
21'-4" x 19'-3"
Vaulted Clg.

Built-ins

Entrainment Center

Lanai

Nook
12'-0" Clg.

Built-in

WH

Optional Valet
Her WIC

Arch

Pool Room

Niche

Arch

Fireplace

Living Room
17'-0" x 23'-2"
12'-0" to 14'-0"
Stepped Ceiling

Arch

Arch

Wet Bar

Arch

Kitchen
17'-0" x 16'-3"
10' Clg.

M. Bath
13'-4" x 13'-9"
12'-0" Stepped Clg.

Niche

His WIC

Arch

Arch

Pantry

Built-ins

WIC

Bath 2

Linen

Niche

Walk-in Shower

Study
14'-5" x 14'-9"
12'-0" to 14'-0"
Stepped Clg.

Built-in

Arch

Foyer
16'-8" Clg.

Niche   Niche

Arch

Dining
14'-0" x 14'-6"
13'-0" to 14'-0"
Stepped Clg.

Arch

Arch

Gallery

Guest Suite 2
13'-3" x 14'-6"
10'-0" Clg.

WIC

Iron Station

SinkSpa

Studio

Duet W/D
DryAire

Guest Suite 1
11'-8" x 15'-0"
10'-0" Clg.

Bath 1

WH

Optional Freezerator

Optional Gladiator System

2 Car Garage
23'-0" x 26'-10"
11'-0" Clg.

Golf Cart

AC

AC

PHOTO ABOVE: *Casual, yet highly efficient, the design of the home's gourmet kitchen gives the chef ready access to up-to-date conveniences.*

PLAN | *6672a Monterray Lane*

3 Bedroom

4 Bath

Width: 79'0"

Depth: 117'2"

Exterior Walls: 8" CBS

Living Area: 4,009 sq ft

Foundation: Slab

Price Code: **PSE5**

Includes Whirlpool® Family Studio

Please note: Home photographed may differ from blueprint.

PLAN | *6921* *Milano*

Photography: Laurence Taylor

PHOTO ABOVE: *In the tradition of Renaissance European design and the villas of Andrea Palladio, this spectacular elevation was designed to bring the outdoors in. Its opulent interior amenities include an octagonal study, circular breakfast nook, library/loft, barrel-vaulted porte-cochere, outdoor kitchen and observation deck — creating an environment that extends beyond walls and balustrades.*

PHOTO RIGHT: *The second-story loft, with its coffered ceiling and spiral staircase, provides access to a third bedroom and media room, as well as a dramatic view of the leisure room below.*

PHOTO FAR RIGHT: *A second-story observation deck graced with open arches and shapely balusters, along with the upper- and lower-level bay windows of the breakfast area and upstairs loft, offer breathtaking views from both first and second story.*

PHOTO ABOVE: *Low-pitched roofs, stately arches and columns, elegant balustrades — these trademarks of Renaissance Revival architecture meet contemporary angled glass and stucco to create a truly unique rear elevation.*

PHOTO RIGHT: *Like a salon in the bow of a splendid ocean liner, the living room's ninety-degree retreating glass doors pierce the evening sky and carry the home's living room out into the brilliant colors of a tropical sunset.*

PHOTO ABOVE: *An outdoor entertainer's paradise complete with outdoor kitchen, the verandah can easily accommodate a party of two hundred or, if you prefer, a party of two.*

PHOTO RIGHT: *Entertaining is once again the theme in the spacious kitchen, which boasts generous portions of everything from food-preparation and pantry space to built-in appliances and breakfast-bar seating.*

PHOTO FAR RIGHT: *The loft can serve as a library or billiard room. In either case, it's a great hangout for friends staying in one or both of the two second-story guest suites.*

80 DAN SATER'S LUXURY HOME PLANS

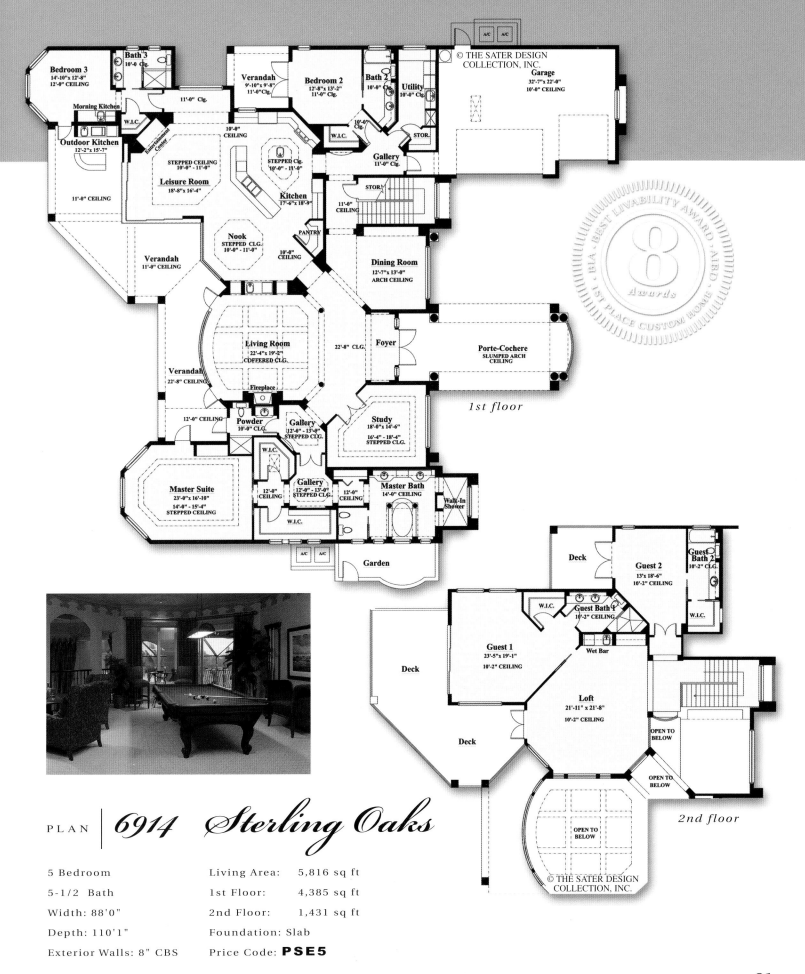

1st floor

© THE SATER DESIGN COLLECTION, INC.

Bedroom 3
14'-10"x 12'-8"
12'-0" CEILING

Bath 3
10'-0" Clg.

Morning Kitchen

W.I.C.

Outdoor Kitchen
12'-2"x 15'-7"

Entertainment Center

11'-0" CEILING

Verandah
9'-10"x 9'-8"
11'-0" Clg.

11'-0" Clg.

Bedroom 2
12'-8"x 13'-2"
11'-0" Clg.

Bath 2
10'-0" Clg.

Utility
10'-0" Clg.

W.I.C.

STOR.

Garage
32'-7"x 22'-0"
10'-0" CEILING

10'-0" CEILING

STEPPED CEILING
10'-0" - 11'-0"

Leisure Room
18'-8"x 16'-4"

STEPPED Clg.
10'-0" - 11'-0"

Kitchen
17'-6"x 18'-9"

Gallery
11'-0" Clg.

STOR.

11'-0" CEILING

Nook
STEPPED CLG.
10'-0" - 11'-0"

PANTRY

10'-0" CEILING

Verandah
11'-0" CEILING

Dining Room
12'-7"x 13'-0"
ARCH CEILING

Living Room
22'-4"x 19'-2"
COFFERED CLG.

22'-8" CLG.

Foyer

Porte-Cochere
SLUMPED ARCH CEILING

Verandah
22'-8" CEILING

Fireplace

12'-0" CEILING

Powder
10'-0" CLG.

Gallery
12'-0" - 13'-0"
STEPPED CLG.

Study
18'-0"x 14'-6"
16'-4" - 18'-4"
STEPPED CLG.

W.I.C.

Master Suite
23'-0"x 16'-10"
14'-0" - 15'-4"
STEPPED CEILING

12'-0" CEILING

Gallery
12'-0" - 13'-0"
STEPPED CLG.

12'-0" CEILING

Master Bath
14'-0" CEILING

Walk-In Shower

W.I.C.

A/C A/C

Garden

2nd floor

Deck

Guest 2
13'x 18'-6"
10'-2" CEILING

Guest Bath 2
10'-2" CLG.

W.I.C.

W.I.C.

Guest Bath
10'-2" CEILING

Deck

Guest 1
23'-5"x 19'-1"
10'-2" CEILING

Wet Bar

Loft
21'-11" x 21'-8"
10'-2" CEILING

OPEN TO BELOW

OPEN TO BELOW

Deck

OPEN TO BELOW

OPEN TO BELOW

© THE SATER DESIGN COLLECTION, INC.

PLAN | *6914 Sterling Oaks*

5 Bedroom

5-1/2 Bath

Width: 88'0"

Depth: 110'1"

Exterior Walls: 8" CBS

Living Area: 5,816 sq ft

1st Floor: 4,385 sq ft

2nd Floor: 1,431 sq ft

Foundation: Slab

Price Code: **PSE5**

Please note: Home photographed may differ from blueprint.

PLAN | *6742 Sherbrooke*

Photography: Laurence Taylor

PHOTO ABOVE: *This unique Mediterranean estate home is nothing less than spectacular. True to its Revival roots — with just a touch of island vernacular — the façade boasts decorative columns, recessed entry, turret, low-pitched hipped roof and cupola. Just as impressive is the home's interior, where volume ceilings and walls of glass create nearly five-thousand square feet of luxurious livability.*

PHOTO RIGHT: *The ideal place for an informal meal or drinks at sunset, this cozy courtyard with outdoor fireplace is conveniently accessible from the leisure room, guest suite and kitchen.*

PHOTO FAR RIGHT: *Children of all ages will enjoy the playful guest retreat at "Camp Grandma." Sliding glass doors offer outdoor fun, while the nearby kitchen offers the possibility of a midnight snack.*

PHOTO ABOVE: *The living room, with access to the lanai via two sets of French doors, is set apart from the dining and foyer area by Tuscan columns and made even more unique by an octagonal ceiling with inlaid wood. Attention to detail is evident throughout, from carved coffers to majestic marble flooring.*

PHOTO RIGHT: *The design elements of the living room flow into the formal dining area in graceful arches, exotic columns paneled with inlaid wood, a high domed ceiling with exposed cypress beams and carved coffers.*

PHOTO ABOVE: *The gourmet kitchen combines state-of-the-art appliances and amenities — hooded range, double ovens, food-preparation center island and marble counter tops — with casual comfort, creating an environment that will surely be a favorite gathering spot.*

PHOTO LEFT: *An outdoor grill, at the far end of a rambling lanai, offers "serious" outdoor dining opportunities, while an observation deck above provides equally serious stargazing.*

PHOTO ABOVE: *On summer evenings, a cool breeze streams in through sliding glass doors, creating the perfect "sleeping weather" in this cheerful master suite.*

TOP PHOTO: *Topped with decorative corbels, a stately, ornately carved partition wall separates the Roman tub from a spacious walk-in shower designed for two. Arch-top windows supply ample panoramas of the master garden.*

PHOTO ABOVE: *The leisure room is the perfect play place for adults with built-in entertainment center, wet bar and nearby kitchen. When guests run out of things to do in the house, they can always be sent out to the courtyard to "play."*

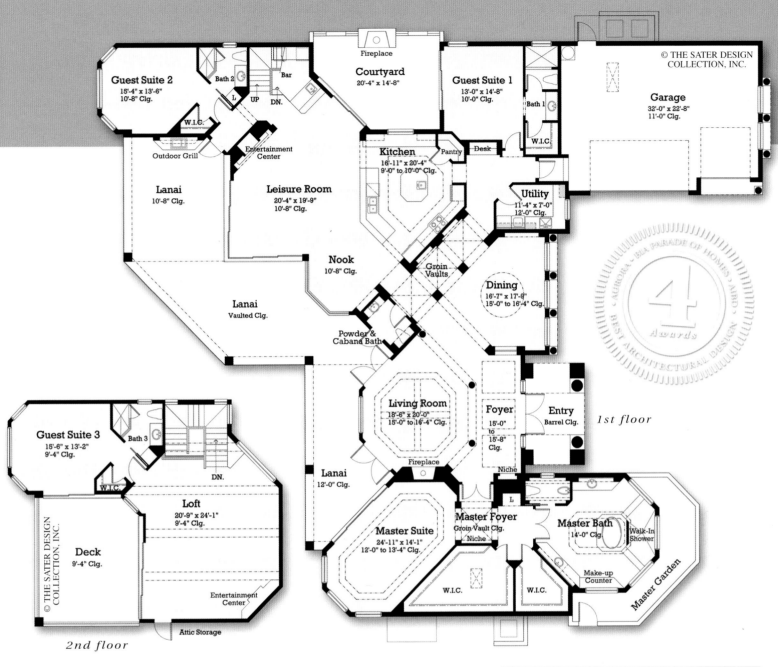

© THE SATER DESIGN COLLECTION, INC.

Guest Suite 2
15'-4" x 13'-6"
10'-8" Clg.

Bath 2

Bar

UP DN.

Fireplace

Courtyard
20'-4" x 14'-8"

Guest Suite 1
13'-0" x 14'-8"
10'-0" Clg.

Bath 1

W.I.C.

Garage
32'-0" x 22'-8"
11'-0" Clg.

W.I.C.

Outdoor Grill

Entertainment Center

Lanai
10'-8" Clg.

Leisure Room
20'-4" x 19'-9"
10'-8" Clg.

Kitchen
16'-11" x 20'-4"
9'-0" to 10'-0" Clg.

Pantry

Desk

Utility
11'-4" x 7'-0"
12'-0" Clg.

Nook
10'-8" Clg.

Groin Vaults

Dining
16'-7" x 17'-8"
15'-0" to 16'-4" Clg.

Lanai
Vaulted Clg.

Powder & Cabana Bath

Living Room
18'-6" x 20'-0"
15'-0" to 16'-4" Clg.

Foyer
15'-0" to 15'-8"

Entry
Barrel Clg.

Niche

1st floor

Fireplace

Lanai
12'-0" Clg.

Master Suite
24'-11" x 14'-1"
12'-0" to 13'-4" Clg.

Master Foyer
Groin Vault Clg.

Niche

Master Bath
14'-0" Clg.

Walk-In Shower

W.I.C.

W.I.C.

Make-up Counter

Master Garden

Guest Suite 3
15'-6" x 13'-2"
9'-4" Clg.

Bath 3

DN.

W.I.C.

Loft
20'-9" x 24'-1"
9'-4" Clg.

© THE SATER DESIGN COLLECTION, INC.

Deck
9'-4" Clg.

Entertainment Center

Attic Storage

2nd floor

PLAN | **6742** *Sherbrooke*

4 Bedroom
4-1/2 Bath
Width: 91'4"
Depth: 109'0"
Exterior Walls: 8" CBS

Living Area: 4,771 sq ft
1st Floor: 3,933 sq ft
2nd Floor: 838 sq ft
Foundation: Slab
Price Code: **PSE5**

PHOTO ABOVE: *Upstairs is the guest room and loft, which serves as an ideal place for a study or den. The adjoining deck offers fresh air and refreshing vistas.*

Please note: Home photographed may differ from blueprint. Not available for construction in Lee or Collier Counties, Florida.

PLAN | *6674a Governor's Club Way*

Photography: RM Designs

PHOTO ABOVE: *Two-toned stucco contrasts brilliantly with a blue summer sky, while slender columns skillfully support a majestic portico entry. Dignified turrets add an air of stature and symmetry. This contemporary Mediterranean villa basks in the afternoon sun, as well as the timeless beauty of Revival-style architectural design.*

PHOTO RIGHT: *Ideal for those with an appetite for spectacular views, this breakfast nook — with buffet server conveniently set in an arched coffer — serves up a serene setting for any mealtime gathering.*

PHOTO ABOVE: *Generous arch-topped built-ins bring not just illumination, but a contemporary sense of style to this highly livable leisure room.*

PHOTO LEFT: *This open kitchen design offers both form and function. The adjacent family studio doubles as a butler's pantry, with space for an optional second freezer.*

PHOTO ABOVE: *The family studio offers, among other things, a fold-down ironing board that takes up zero floor space, and the SinkSpa™, a jetted sink that performs gentle-care washings with ease.*

PHOTO ABOVE: *A totally new concept in home planning, the Family Studio is a place that's designed to make your life easier, and every day more productive. Each Whirlpool® appliance is compact, reliable and efficient.*

PHOTO ABOVE: *The highlight of the master suite, this walk-in closet — one of two — is outfitted with the latest in garment care technology from Whirlpool®: an ImPress™ Ironing Station and a DryAire™ Drying Cabinet, which provides easy, gentle garment care.*

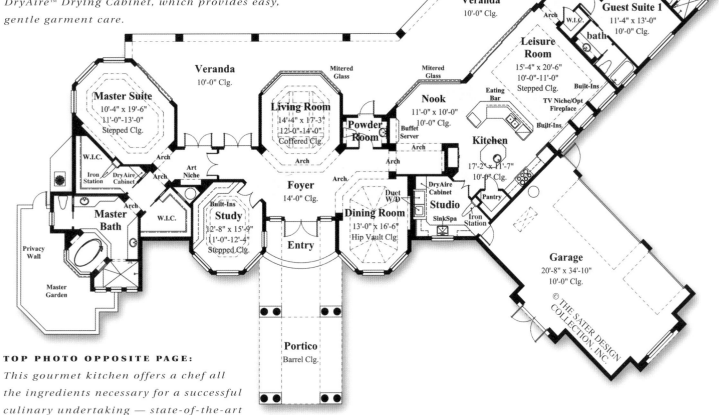

TOP PHOTO OPPOSITE PAGE:

This gourmet kitchen offers a chef all the ingredients necessary for a successful culinary undertaking — state-of-the-art KitchenAid® appliances that meet the desires of the passionate cook.

PLAN | *6674a Governor's Club Way*

3 Bedroom

3-1/2 Bath

Width: 121'5"

Depth: 96'2"

Exterior Walls: 8" CBS

Living Area: 3,398 sq ft

Foundation: Slab

Price Code: **C4**

Includes Whirlpool® Family Studio

Please note: Home photographed may differ from blueprint.

Photography: Laurence Taylor

PHOTO ABOVE: *Welcome to your own personal Caribbean-island paradise resort! This British Colonial-inspired design glimmers in the early evening twilight, with illuminated entry turret and cupola sparkling like beacons to guide its owners safely home.*

PHOTO RIGHT: *The foyer — replete with carved coffer, paneled decorative columns and vaulted ceiling — makes every entrance a grand one.*

PHOTO ABOVE: *Curtains at the far end of the spacious living room are drawn back to reveal a beautiful landscape beyond zero-corner glass doors and the lanai. Like a tremendous, unframed work of art, the landscape image serves as both the focal point and inspiration for the interior design.*

PHOTO LEFT: *An abundance of built-ins in the study provides generous real estate for books — which doesn't mean, however, that this isn't a perfect room for simply catching a cat nap on the comfortable sofa.*

PHOTO ABOVE: *The Spanish vernacular is evident in the covered courtyard's festive, "hacienda-style" outdoor kitchen and fireplace sitting area — its boundaries punctuated by stately Tuscan columns.*

PHOTO ABOVE: *Morning sunlight streams into the breakfast nook, graced with semi-circular, floor-to-ceiling windows.*

PHOTO ABOVE: *Why not make your life, or the butler's, a little easier? To facilitate serving guests, this plan includes a butler's pantry that conveniently connects the formal dining area to the gourmet kitchen.*

PHOTO ABOVE: *The lateral arrangement between leisure room and kitchen, with nearby breakfast nook, creates a "casual zone" — a great place for relaxing with friends and snacks.*

PHOTO LEFT: *Gorgeous sunset views are abundant, including this one of the home's rear elevation at twilight.*

PHOTO ABOVE: *There's a little bit of country in this casual kitchen, with its cheerful, natural-light-bearing windows, butcher-block center island and airy appeal.*

PHOTO RIGHT: *The leisure room is casual and comfortable, spacious yet intimate. The glow from a unique, illuminated volume ceiling warms the room.*

Courtyard
18'-6" x 34'-0"

Outdoor Kitchen

Fireplace

Storage

Lanai
12'-0" Clg.

Entertainment Center

Leisure Room
20'-8" x 22'-11"
Vaulted Clg.

Built-Ins

Lanai
10'-4" Clg.

Sitting Room

Lanai
12'-0" Clg.

Master Suite
14'-6" x 21'-0"
12'-0"-13'-4" Clg.

Nook
11'-0" x 13'-0"
12'-0" Clg.

Server

Kitchen
16'-0" x 16'-10"
10'-0" Clg

Pwdr.

Living Room
14'-6" x 21'-0"
14'-0" Clg.

Fireplace

Pool Bath

Master Foyer

WIC

Butler

Pantry

Master Bath

WIC

Linen

Bath 1

WIC

Buffet

Walk-In Shower

Dn.

Foyer

Bath No. 3

W.I.C.

Bonus Room
14'-0" x 18'-0"

© THE SATER DESIGN COLLECTION, INC.

balcony

2nd floor

Guest Suite 1
12'-0" x 15'-3"
10'-0" Clg.

Dining Room
16'-0" x 15'-0"
13'-0"-14'-0" Clg.

Foyer
Groin Vault Clg.

Built-Ins

Study
14'-0" x 17'-0"
12'-0"-12'-6" Clg.

Built-Ins

Master Garden

Utility
8'-4" x 9'-6"

Gallery

Closet

Up

Dn.

Bath 2

Guest Suite 2
12'-6" x 17'-0"
10'-0" Clg.

Walk-In Shower

Entry

Built-Ins

1st floor

Garage
23'-8" x 32'-4"
9'-0" Clg.

© THE SATER DESIGN COLLECTION, INC.

PLAN | *6927* *Andros Island*

3 Bedroom

4-1/2 Bath

Width: 98'5"

Depth: 125'11"

Exterior Walls: 8" CBS

Living Area: 5,169 sq ft

1st Floor: 4,604 sq ft

2nd Floor: 565 sq ft

Foundation: Slab

Price Code: **PSE5**

Please note: Home photographed may differ from blueprint.

Photography: Laurence Taylor

PHOTO ABOVE: *Sun-drenched stucco and red barrel tile, along with extensive use of the Roman arch, are hallmarks of Spanish influence on American architectural design. This history-rich villa demonstrates that heritage in the grandest of ways, as it basks in the glory of the mid-afternoon sun.*

PHOTO RIGHT: *Volume ceilings throughout add dramatic dimension to the interior space. Here in the living room, that drama is further enhanced by a trio of floor-to-ceiling windows.*

PHOTO ABOVE: *The living room transitions seamlessly into a formal dining area. Decorative columns support graceful arches, as well as two soaring stepped ceilings.*

PHOTO RIGHT: *There's nothing quite like a comfortable kitchen — which is exactly what this one is — not only for preparing meals but for gathering and conversing.*

PHOTO ABOVE: *This view of the leisure room and kitchen from the lanai provides proof that sliding glass doors can offer spectacular views, not just of the exterior landscape, but the interior as well.*

PHOTO ABOVE: *To add a cool lanai breeze to this cozy master suite, simply open the retreating glass doors.*

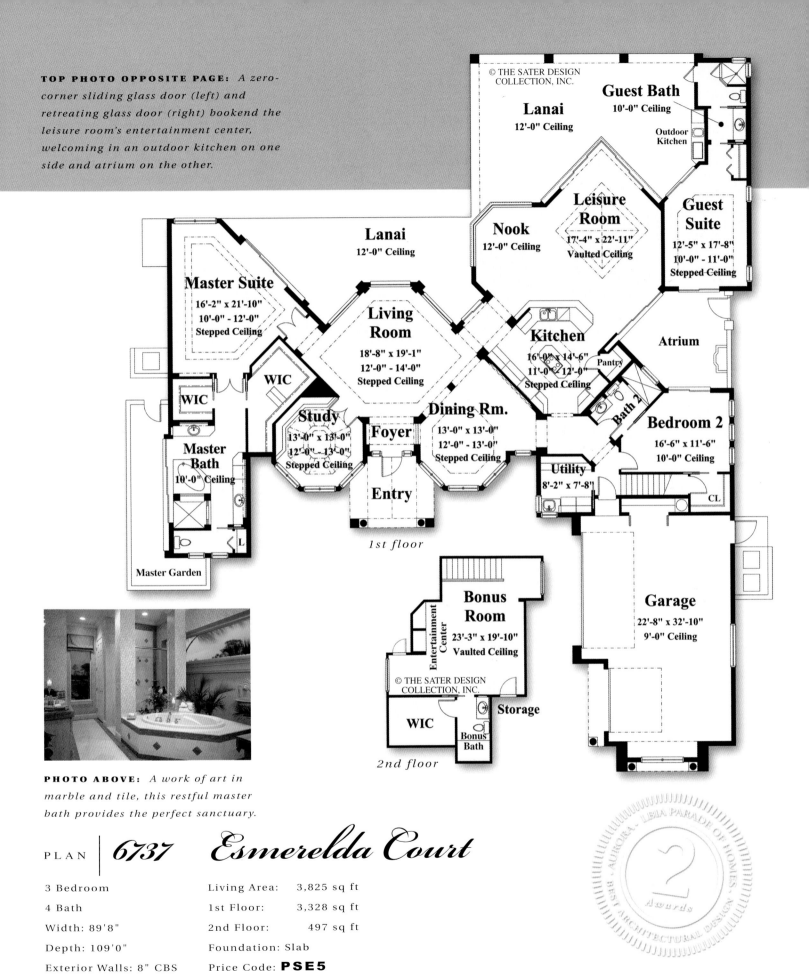

TOP PHOTO OPPOSITE PAGE: *A zero-corner sliding glass door (left) and retreating glass door (right) bookend the leisure room's entertainment center, welcoming in an outdoor kitchen on one side and atrium on the other.*

© THE SATER DESIGN COLLECTION, INC.

Lanai
12'-0" Ceiling

Guest Bath
10'-0" Ceiling

Outdoor Kitchen

Leisure Room
17'-4" x 22'-11"
Vaulted Ceiling

Nook
12'-0" Ceiling

Guest Suite
12'-5" x 17'-8"
10'-0" - 11'-0"
Stepped Ceiling

Lanai
12'-0" Ceiling

Master Suite
16'-2" x 21'-10"
10'-0" - 12'-0"
Stepped Ceiling

Living Room
18'-8" x 19'-1"
12'-0" - 14'-0"
Stepped Ceiling

Kitchen
16'-0" x 14'-6"
11'-0" - 12'-0"
Stepped Ceiling

Atrium

WIC

WIC

Study
13'-0" x 13'-0"
12'-0" - 13'-0"
Stepped Ceiling

Foyer

Dining Rm.
13'-0" x 13'-0"
12'-0" - 13'-0"
Stepped Ceiling

Pantry

Bath 2

Bedroom 2
16'-6" x 11'-6"
10'-0" Ceiling

Master Bath
10'-0" Ceiling

Entry

Utility
8'-2" x 7'-8"

CL

Master Garden

1st floor

Bonus Room
23'-3" x 19'-10"
Vaulted Ceiling

Entertainment Center

Garage
22'-8" x 32'-10"
9'-0" Ceiling

© THE SATER DESIGN COLLECTION, INC.

WIC

Bonus Bath

Storage

2nd floor

PHOTO ABOVE: *A work of art in marble and tile, this restful master bath provides the perfect sanctuary.*

PLAN | *6737* *Esmerelda Court*

3 Bedroom

4 Bath

Width: 89'8"

Depth: 109'0"

Exterior Walls: 8" CBS

Living Area: 3,825 sq ft

1st Floor: 3,328 sq ft

2nd Floor: 497 sq ft

Foundation: Slab

Price Code: **PSE5**

Please note: Home photographed may differ from blueprint.
Not available for construction in Lee or Collier Counties, Florida.

Photography: Everett & Soulé

PHOTO ABOVE: *Like a cat stretching out in his favorite sunny spot, this eye-catching, Southern contemporary home just basks in the sun, settling comfortably into its tropical surroundings. An elegant porte-cochere and stylish barrel dormer add touches of lavishness, but the home still retains its easy-going disposition.*

PHOTO RIGHT: *The formal dining room, with its opulent, octagonal step ceiling, boasts an adjacent wet bar and ample natural light from a trio of front-facing bay windows.*

PHOTO FAR RIGHT: *Reminiscent of an ancient pyramid, a great, carved-stone fireplace with tapered chimney warms the spacious living room. Complementing the massive hearth is a pair of stone Tuscan columns, stoically bearing the burden of an impressive arch.*

PHOTO ABOVE: *Your guests may never even get to their room. Both this cozy fireplace sitting area and handy outdoor kitchen are conveniently located just outside the guest suite.*

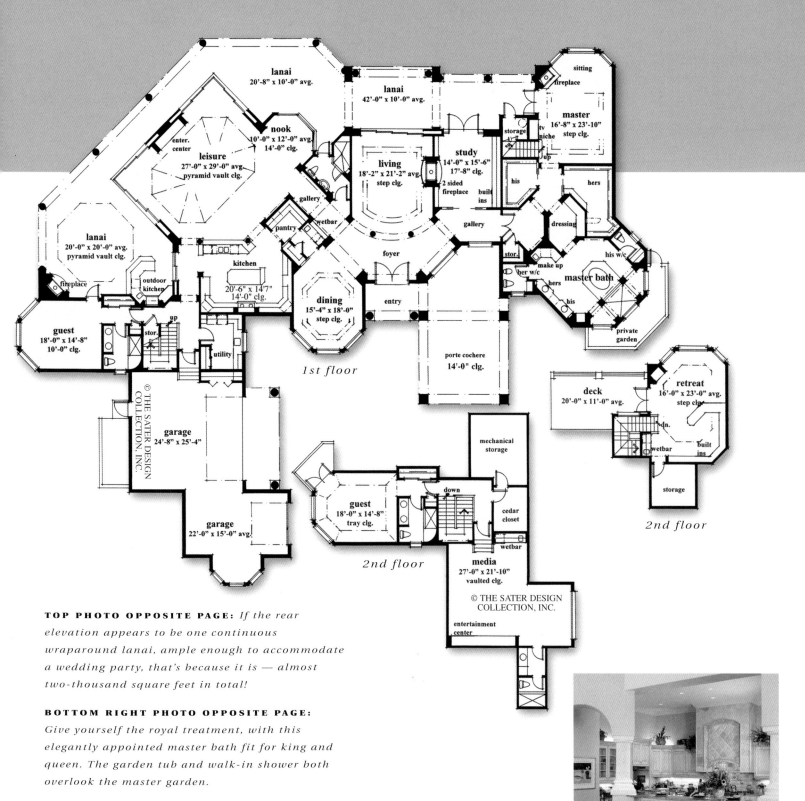

1st floor

2nd floor

2nd floor

© THE SATER DESIGN COLLECTION, INC.

© THE SATER DESIGN COLLECTION, INC.

TOP PHOTO OPPOSITE PAGE: *If the rear elevation appears to be one continuous wraparound lanai, ample enough to accommodate a wedding party, that's because it is — almost two-thousand square feet in total!*

BOTTOM RIGHT PHOTO OPPOSITE PAGE: *Give yourself the royal treatment, with this elegantly appointed master bath fit for king and queen. The garden tub and walk-in shower both overlook the master garden.*

PLAN | *6900* *Huntington Lakes*

3 Bedroom	Living Area: 6,770 sq ft
4 Bath	1st Floor: 5,170 sq ft
Width: 140'7"	2nd Floor: 1,600 sq ft
Depth: 118'4"	Foundation: Slab
Exterior Walls: 8" CBS	Price Code: **PSE5**

PHOTO ABOVE: *Don't let the casual comfort of this kitchen fool you. It offers the serious chef every state-of-the-art food-preparation amenity under the sun.*

Please note: Home photographed may differ from blueprint.

Photography: Laurence Taylor

PHOTO ABOVE: *Picture perfect, this spectacular Colonial Revival manor home is truly one of a kind. While design elements evident in the façade, such as balustrades, cupolas, turrets, hipped roofs and barrel tile, harken the home back to Revival roots, its interior takes a decidedly contemporary turn.*

PHOTO RIGHT: *A carved coffer provides a nice niche for a server, while the arched ceiling serves as the perfect complement to a gorgeous arch-top window in this marvelously modern formal dining area.*

PHOTO ABOVE: *Soft lighting and mellow colors exude warmth in the foyer and formal dining area. The architectural language of the ancient Greeks takes a 21st-century turn, evident in the sleek arches supported by tapered columns.*

PHOTO LEFT: *This home's spectacular leisure room goes where no home has gone before in terms of welcoming the outside in. With zero-corner glass doors open, an entire wall disappears, highlighting the magnificent free-standing entertainment center against the lush greens and blues of the landscape beyond.*

PHOTO ABOVE: *The wet bar is open... to both the dining area and the gourmet kitchen. Rich, dark wood, recessed panels and recessed lighting provide a "cigar bar" sophistication to this entertainer's dream.*

PHOTO RIGHT: *Contemporary conveniences — expansive counter space, food-prep center island and double sinks, to name just a few — abound in this casual, yet state-of-the-art kitchen.*

PHOTO FAR RIGHT: *Once again, Mediterranean meets modern — this time in the spacious master bath. The walk-in shower and whirlpool bath echo the architecture of the ancients and are complemented by the futuristic use of glass and lighting.*

PHOTO ABOVE: *Zero-corner glass doors and expansive windows in the master suite allow this space to stretch outward, encompassing both the wraparound veranda on one side and the master garden on the other.*

PHOTO RIGHT: *Kitchen, nook and leisure room — as well as veranda via retreating glass doors — come together to create this spacious, family-friendly "common zone."*

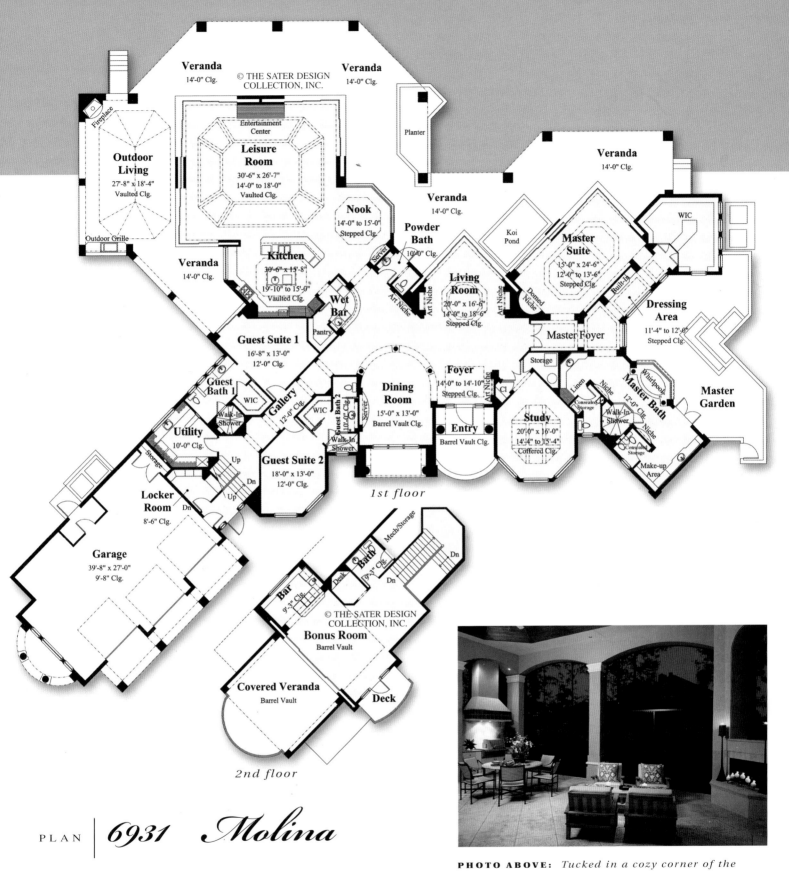

© THE SATER DESIGN
COLLECTION, INC.

Veranda
14'-0" Clg.

Veranda
14'-0" Clg.

Planter

Veranda
14'-0" Clg.

Fireplace

Entertainment
Center

Outdoor
Living
27'-8" x 18'-4"
Vaulted Clg.

Leisure
Room
30'-6" x 26'-7"
14'-0" to 18'-0"
Vaulted Clg.

Nook
14'-0" to 15'-0"
Stepped Clg.

Powder
Bath
10'-0" Clg.

Koi
Pond

Master
Suite
15'-0" x 24'-6"
12'-0" to 13'-6"
Stepped Clg.

WIC

Outdoor Grille

Veranda
14'-0" Clg.

Kitchen
30'-6" x 15'-8"
19'-10" to 15'-0"
Vaulted Clg.

Server

Living
Room
20'-0" x 16'-6"
14'-0" to 18'-6"
Stepped Clg.

Art Niche

Art Niche

Domed
Niche

Built-In

Dressing
Area
11'-4" to 12'-0"
Stepped Clg.

Wet
Bar

Master Foyer

Whirlpool

Guest Suite 1
16'-8" x 13'-0"
12'-0" Clg.

Pantry

Storage

Cl

Storage

Linen

Niche

Master
Bath
12'-0" Clg.

Master
Garden

Guest
Bath 1

WIC

Gallery
12'-0" Clg.

Guest Bath 2
10'-0" Clg.

WIC

Dining
Room
15'-0" x 13'-0"
Barrel Vault Clg.

Server

Foyer
14'-0" to 14'-10"
Stepped Clg.

Art Niche

Entry
Barrel Vault Clg.

Study
20'-0" x 16'-0"
14'-4" to 15'-4"
Coffered Clg.

Concealed
Storage

Walk-In
Shower

Niche

Make-up
Area

Concealed
Storage

Walk-In
Shower

Utility
10'-0" Clg.

Storage

Walk-In
Shower

Guest Suite 2
18'-0" x 13'-0"
12'-0" Clg.

Up

Dn

Up

1st floor

Locker
Room
8'-6" Clg.

Dn

Garage
39'-8" x 27'-0"
9'-8" Clg.

Bar
9'-3" Clg.

Bath
9'-3" Clg.

Desk

Mech/Storage

Dn

Dn

© THE SATER DESIGN
COLLECTION, INC.

Bonus Room
Barrel Vault

Covered Veranda
Barrel Vault

Deck

2nd floor

PLAN | *6931* *Molina*

3 Bedroom

4-1/2 Bath

Width: 146'0"

Depth: 132'5"

Exterior Walls: 8" CBS

Living Area: 6,340 sq ft

1st Floor: 5,696 sq ft

2nd Floor: 644 sq ft

Foundation: Slab

Price Code: **PSE5**

PHOTO ABOVE: *Tucked in a cozy corner of the spacious outdoor living room, an outdoor kitchen serves as a comfortable place for a casual meal.*

Please note: Home photographed may differ from blueprint.

Photography: Laurence Taylor

PHOTO ABOVE: *A richly stated recessed entry serves as both grand entrance and focal point for the façade of this British Colonial-style resort home. Decorative columns stand guard on either side of this classic approach, culminating in a set of mile-high double doors.*

PHOTO RIGHT: *A deeply carved coffer, ornate moldings, soaring octagonal ceiling and floor-to-ceiling bay window are some of the fine architectural features that make the dining room a beautiful backdrop for formal gatherings.*

PHOTO ABOVE: *Elegant yet sturdy, ten-foot columns support soft slump arches, loosely defining the living room and generous dining room beyond. To the right, the grotto awaits behind two sets of wrought-iron gates.*

PHOTO LEFT: *Nook, leisure room and kitchen converge to create a spacious — and gracious — living area. Courtesy of zero-corner glass doors, spectacular exterior vistas become part of the equally spectacular interior landscape.*

PHOTO ABOVE: *Like sentries, statuesque columns stand guard at the boundary between indoor and outdoor space. An outdoor kitchen (visible to left) is just outside the leisure room, and offers a great place to gather for snacks and drinks.*

PHOTO FAR RIGHT: *Carved double doors and an ornate barrel-vault ceiling are hallmarks of this stately foyer.*

PHOTO ABOVE: *The grotto makes an ideal wine cellar. A unique groin-vaulted ceiling and wrought-iron gates create an ideal "temporary resting place" for favorite wines.*

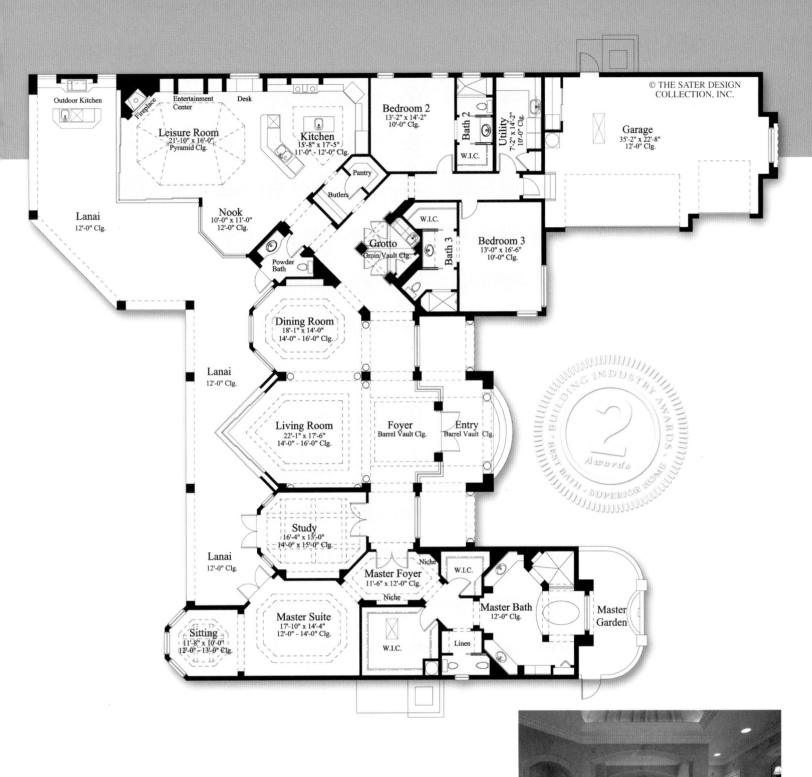

Outdoor Kitchen

Fireplace

Entertainment Center

Desk

© THE SATER DESIGN COLLECTION, INC.

Leisure Room
21'-10" x 16'-0"
Pyramid Clg.

Kitchen
15'-8" x 17'-5"
11'-0" - 12'-0" Clg.

Bedroom 2
13'-2" x 14'-2"
10'-0" Clg.

Bath 2

Utility
7'-2" x 14'-2"
10'-0" Clg.

Garage
35'-2" x 22'-8"
12'-0" Clg.

Lanai
12'-0" Clg.

Nook
10'-0" x 11'-0"
12'-0" Clg.

Pantry

Butlers

W.I.C.

W.I.C.

Powder Bath

Grotto
Groin/Vault Clg.

Bath 3

Bedroom 3
13'-0" x 16'-6"
10'-0" Clg.

Dining Room
18'-1" x 14'-0"
14'-0" - 16'-0" Clg.

Lanai
12'-0" Clg.

Living Room
22'-1" x 17'-6"
14'-0" - 16'-0" Clg.

Foyer
Barrel Vault Clg.

Entry
Barrel Vault Clg.

BUILDING INDUSTRY AWARDS · BEST BATH · SUPERIOR HOME ·
2 Awards

Lanai
12'-0" Clg.

Study
16'-4" x 13'-0"
14'-0" x 15'-0" Clg.

Niche

W.I.C.

Master Foyer
11'-6" x 12'-0" Clg.

Niche

W.I.C.

Master Bath
12'-0" Clg.

Master Garden

Lanai
12'-0" Clg.

Sitting
11'-8" x 10'-0"
12'-0" - 13'-0" Clg.

Master Suite
17'-10" x 14'-4"
12'-0" - 14'-0" Clg.

W.I.C.

Linen

PLAN | *6907* *Monticello*

3 Bedroom

3-1/2 Bath

Width: 91'6"

Depth: 117'0"

Exterior Walls: 8" CBS

Living Area: 4,255 sq ft

Foundation: Slab

Price Code: **PSE5**

Please note: Home photographed may differ from blueprint.

PHOTO ABOVE: *The oval garden tub of the master bath, with its private view of the master garden, restores, refreshes and rejuvenates.*

PLAN | *6653a Wentworth Trail*

Photography: Laurence Taylor

PHOTO ABOVE: *Classic meets contemporary in this majestic manor home. Brick and stucco, decorative columns and arch-top windows create a street presence that is both traditional and charming. The result? A home that, whether seaside or mountainside, "completes" rather than "competes" with its setting.*

PHOTO RIGHT: *A fourteen-foot ceiling rises above the living room, while zero-corner glass sliding doors open onto a breezy lanai. Together, they give the living room an air of spacious elegance.*

PHOTO ABOVE: *All of the ingredients are here for a terrific gourmet kitchen — built-in refrigerator and double ovens, a cook-top island, easy-clean counter and sink, walk-in pantry and breakfast bar for four.*

PHOTO LEFT: *A breezy lanai, measuring nearly six-hundred square feet, wraps the rear elevation in open-air-entertainment space. Guests will love gathering in the outdoor kitchen and sitting area, directly below the second-story observation deck.*

PHOTO ABOVE: *Discover your own private oasis in this glorious master bath, complete with his-and-her vanities and a cozy master garden-view tub.*

PHOTO ABOVE: *First thing in the morning and last thing at night, spectacular panoramic views are conveniently available through the expanse of windows that wraps the master suite.*

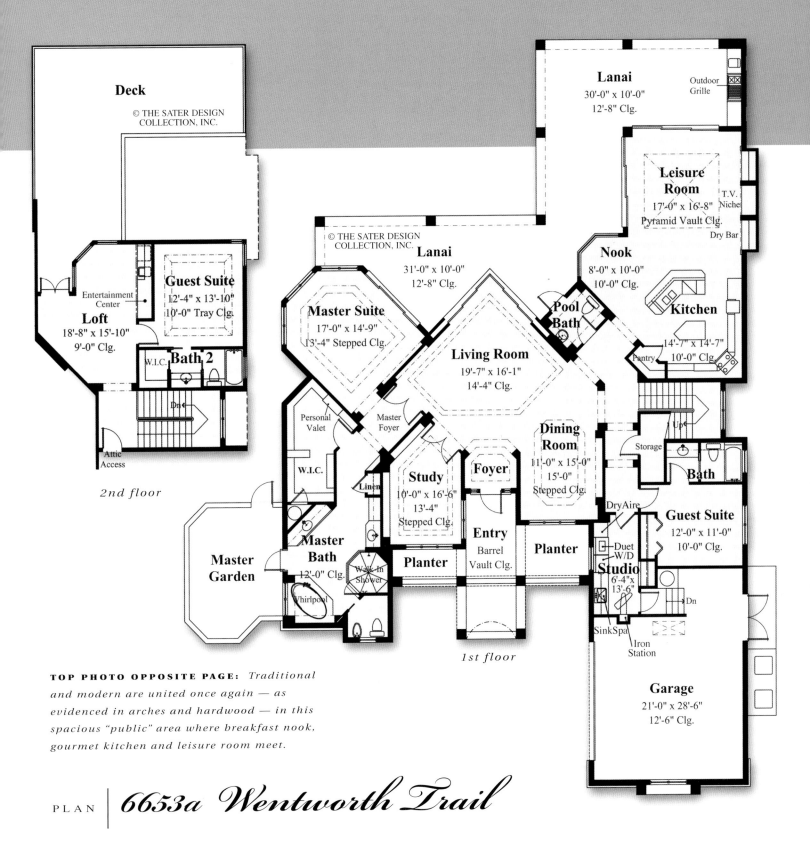

Deck

© THE SATER DESIGN
COLLECTION, INC.

Guest Suite
12'-4" x 13'-10"
10'-0" Tray Clg.

Entertainment
Center

Loft
18'-8" x 15'-10"
9'-0" Clg.

W.I.C. **Bath 2**

Dn

Attic
Access

2nd floor

Lanai
30'-0" x 10'-0"
12'-8" Clg.

Outdoor
Grille

Leisure Room
17'-0" x 16'-8"
Pyramid Vault Clg.

T.V.
Niche

Dry Bar

Nook
8'-0" x 10'-0"
10'-0" Clg.

Kitchen
14'-7" x 14'-7"
10'-0" Clg.

Pantry

© THE SATER DESIGN
COLLECTION, INC.

Lanai
31'-0" x 10'-0"
12'-8" Clg.

Master Suite
17'-0" x 14'-9"
13'-4" Stepped Clg.

Pool Bath

Living Room
19'-7" x 16'-1"
14'-4" Clg.

Personal
Valet

Master
Foyer

Dining Room
11'-0" x 15'-0"
15'-0"
Stepped Clg.

Up

Storage

W.I.C.

Linen

Study
10'-0" x 16'-6"
13'-4"
Stepped Clg.

Foyer

Bath

DryAire

Master Garden

Master Bath
12'-0" Clg.

Walk-In
Shower

Whirlpool

Entry
Barrel
Vault Clg.

Planter

Planter

Duet
W/D

Guest Suite
12'-0" x 11'-0"
10'-0" Clg.

Studio
6'-4" x 13'-6"

SinkSpa

Iron
Station

Dn

1st floor

Garage
21'-0" x 28'-6"
12'-6" Clg.

TOP PHOTO OPPOSITE PAGE: *Traditional and modern are united once again — as evidenced in arches and hardwood — in this spacious "public" area where breakfast nook, gourmet kitchen and leisure room meet.*

PLAN | *6653a Wentworth Trail*

3 Bedroom

3-1/2 Bath

Width: 67'0"

Depth: 102'0"

Exterior Walls: 8" CBS

Living Area: 3,462 sq ft

1st Floor: 2,894 sq ft

2nd Floor: 568 sq ft

Foundation: Slab

Price Code: **C4**

Includes Whirlpool® Family Studio

Please note: Home photographed may differ from blueprint.

Photography: Oscar Thompson

PHOTO ABOVE: *Like a quartet of arrows, glowing gold and pointing upward into the night sky, the façade of this earthly masterpiece — dominated by triangular shapes — makes a bold statement, even at dusk. Materials taken from nature — stacked stone of terracotta and slate, plus various hardwoods — are elemental throughout, creating a look that is reminiscent of the great lodges of America's Pacific Northwest.*

PHOTO RIGHT: *A harmony of wood and stone come together in a rough-hewn yet elegant testament to American craftsmanship and artistry.*

PHOTO FAR RIGHT: *The living room celebrates the grandeur of nature, capturing the beauty and majesty of the great outdoors in stacked-stone columns and hardwood ceiling. A trio of windows stand like the silhouette of angular purple mountains in the background.*

PHOTO ABOVE: *The octagonal formal dining room appears to float on water. Stacked-stone columns, barely in view, stand on the perimeter framing the serene rear view.*

PHOTO RIGHT: *Triangular shapes make their way from the façade to the interior living space, turning ordinary entryways between rooms into grand passageways between adventures.*

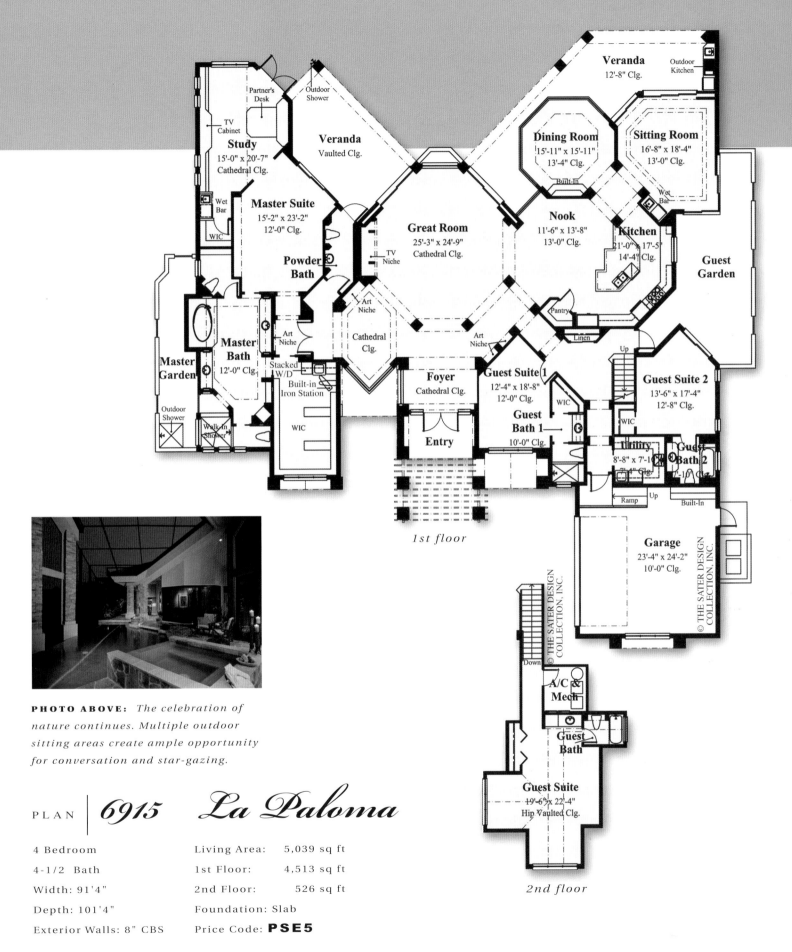

1st floor

2nd floor

© THE SATER DESIGN COLLECTION, INC.

PHOTO ABOVE: *The celebration of nature continues. Multiple outdoor sitting areas create ample opportunity for conversation and star-gazing.*

PLAN | *6915* | *La Paloma*

4 Bedroom

4-1/2 Bath

Width: 91'4"

Depth: 101'4"

Exterior Walls: 8" CBS

Living Area: 5,039 sq ft

1st Floor: 4,513 sq ft

2nd Floor: 526 sq ft

Foundation: Slab

Price Code: **PSE5**

Please note: Home photographed may differ from blueprint.
Not available for construction in Lee or Collier Counties, Florida.

Photography: William C. Minarich

PHOTO ABOVE: *About 450 years ago, the country houses of Andrea Palladio — called "villas" — began to appear in the countryside of the Veneto, the mainland province around Venice. This magnificent home is evocative of those villas. Its five-part profile and entry portico, at one time known as a "barchesse" or farm building, are signature elements of the homes Palladio designed for his patrician patrons.*

PHOTO RIGHT: *The post-Renaissance desire for balance, harmony and grand scale are seen throughout the home, beginning in the formal dining area, where the soaring stepped ceiling is counterbalanced by delicate architectural details.*

PHOTO ABOVE: *In the tradition of harmonious design, the gourmet kitchen must meet three criteria. It must be magnificent, comfortable and functional. This one meets all three, beautifully.*

PHOTO LEFT: *One can stand virtually anywhere in a Palladian home and have a sense of the entire structure, Today, that's referred to as a "transparent" floor plan, as evidenced in this "public area" where leisure room, kitchen and breakfast nook meet.*

PHOTO ABOVE: *Curved-glass bay windows envelop the breakfast nook with a panoramic vista of lush landscape.*

PHOTO ABOVE: *The centerpiece of the formal living room is the grand hearth, with its ornately carved mantel supported by decorative corbels.*

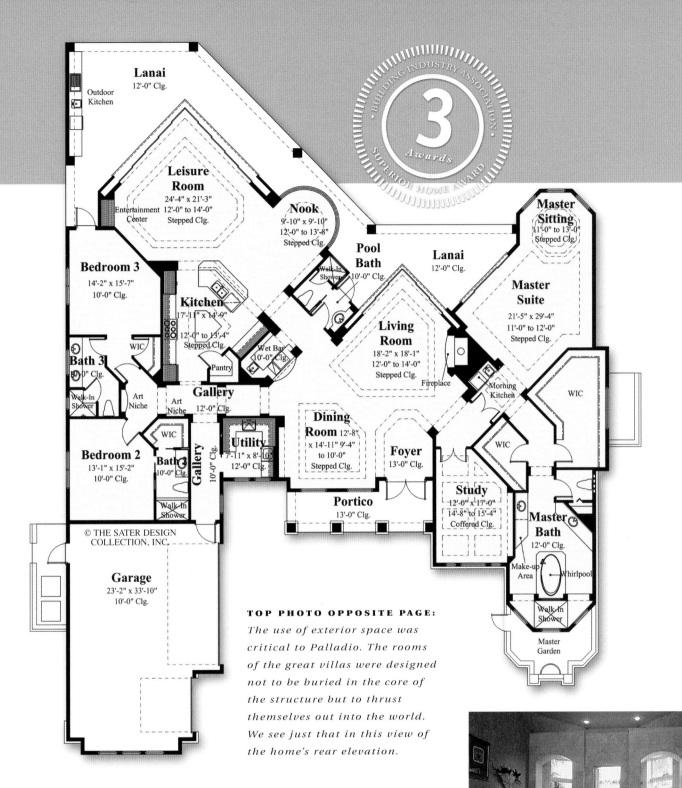

3 Awards — BUILDING INDUSTRY ASSOCIATION · SUPERIOR HOME AWARD

Lanai
12'-0" Clg.

Outdoor Kitchen

Leisure Room
24'-4" x 21'-3"
Entertainment Center 12'-0" to 14'-0"
Stepped Clg.

Nook
9'-10" x 9'-10"
12'-0" to 13'-8"
Stepped Clg.

Pool Bath
10'-0" Clg.
Walk-In Shower

Lanai
12'-0" Clg.

Master Sitting
11'-0" to 13'-0"
Stepped Clg.

Bedroom 3
14'-2" x 15'-7"
10'-0" Clg.

Kitchen
17'-11" x 14'-9"
12'-0" to 13'-4"
Stepped Clg.

Wet Bar
10'-0"

Master Suite
21'-5" x 29'-4"
11'-0" to 12'-0"
Stepped Clg.

Living Room
18'-2" x 18'-1"
12'-0" to 14'-0"
Stepped Clg.

Fireplace

Morning Kitchen

WIC

Bath 3
10'-0" Clg.
Walk-In Shower

WIC

Pantry

Art Niche

Gallery
12'-0" Clg.

Art Niche

Dining Room
12'-8" x 14'-11"
9'-4" to 10'-0"
Stepped Clg.

Foyer
13'-0" Clg.

WIC

Gallery
10'-0" Clg.

Bedroom 2
13'-1" x 15'-2"
10'-0" Clg.

Bath
10'-0" Clg.

WIC

Utility
7'-11" x 8'-0"
12'-0" Clg.

Walk-In Shower

Study
12'-0" x 17'-0"
14'-8" to 15'-4"
Coffered Clg.

Master Bath
12'-0" Clg.

Make-up Area

Whirlpool

© THE SATER DESIGN COLLECTION, INC.

Garage
23'-2" x 33'-10"
10'-0" Clg.

Portico
13'-0" Clg.

Walk-In Shower

Master Garden

TOP PHOTO OPPOSITE PAGE:
The use of exterior space was critical to Palladio. The rooms of the great villas were designed not to be buried in the core of the structure but to thrust themselves out into the world. We see just that in this view of the home's rear elevation.

PLAN | *8034* *Winthrop*

3 Bedroom
4 Bath
Width: 83'10"
Depth: 106'0"
Exterior Walls: 2X6

Living Area: 3,954 sq ft
Foundation: Slab
Price Code: **L1**

Please note: Home photographed may differ from blueprint.

PHOTO ABOVE: *Symmetrical arches add grace, serenity and splendor to a master bath replete with an oversize whirlpool tub and walk-in shower for two.*

Photography: Oscar Thompson

PHOTO ABOVE: *This home is ideal for the homeowner who appreciates melding the old and the new, combining natural surroundings with a comfortable interior. The grand entry, for instance, harbors a wooden arbor trellis and the rear elevation provides a primer on how to incorporate the exterior landscape into interior space.*

PHOTO TOP RIGHT: *A spacious, covered veranda is united with the leisure room via zero-corner sliding glass doors. Bringing together an outdoor kitchen and sitting area, it's the ideal locale for outdoor entertaining.*

PHOTO BOTTOM RIGHT: *Either studio or guest suite — depending on one's needs — this cozy, free-standing space is joined to the home by a covered walkway.*

PHOTO ABOVE: *In the style of a grand rotunda, the formal dining room's eight-foot-high curved wall of glass affords dinner guests an opportunity to enjoy both a magnificent meal and a magnificent view.*

PHOTO LEFT: *A dignified gallery of arches and rusticated columns provides passage between the breakfast nook and the formal living room. To the right is the stairway leading to the second-story loft.*

PHOTO ABOVE: *The "high point" of the rear elevation, a second-story observation deck, presides over the expansive backyard landscape, bounded by a wrought-iron baluster that is as fashionable as it is functional.*

PHOTO RIGHT: *The love affair with the outdoors continues: A two-story stepped ceiling sets a grand and spacious stage for the star performer — a two-story window of curved glass — that acts like a giant screen presenting a magnificent view of the outside world.*

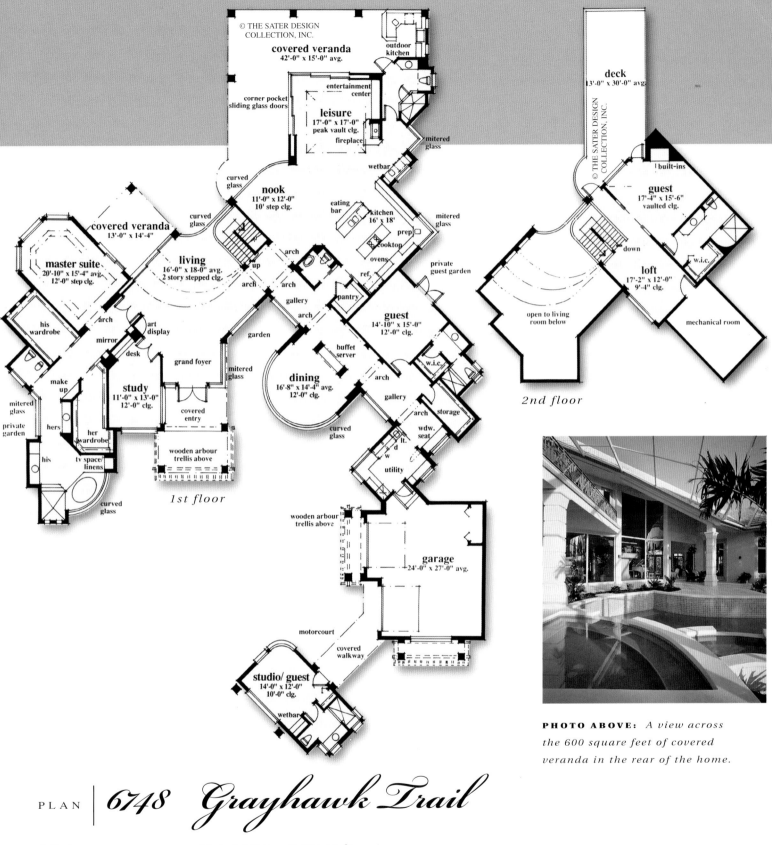

© THE SATER DESIGN
COLLECTION, INC.

covered veranda
42'-0" x 15'-0" avg.

outdoor kitchen

entertainment center

leisure
17'-0" x 17'-0"
peak vault clg.

fireplace

corner pocket
sliding glass doors

mitered glass

wetbar

deck
13'-0" x 30'-0" avg.

© THE SATER DESIGN
COLLECTION, INC.

built-ins

guest
17'-4" x 15'-6"
vaulted clg.

w.i.c.

curved glass

nook
11'-0" x 12'-0"
10' step clg.

eating bar

kitchen
16' x 18'

prep

mitered glass

down

loft
17'-2" x 12'-0"
9'-4" clg.

covered veranda
13'-0" x 14'-4"

curved glass

living
16'-0" x 18'-0" avg.
2 story stepped clg.

arch

up

cooktop

ovens

ref.

private guest garden

open to living
room below

master suite
20'-10" x 15'-4" avg.
12'-0" step clg.

his wardrobe

arch

art display

mirror

desk

arch

arch

gallery

pantry

garden

guest
14'-10" x 15'-0"
12'-0" clg.

arch

w.i.c.

mechanical room

2nd floor

make up

study
11'-0" x 13'-0"
12'-0" clg.

grand foyer

mitered glass

buffet server

arch

mitered glass

hers

her wardrobe

covered entry

dining
16'-8" x 14'-4" avg.
12'-0" clg.

gallery

arch

storage

private garden

his

tv space/ linens

wooden arbour
trellis above

1st floor

curved glass

arch

wdw. seat

curved glass

w
d
lt.

utility

wooden arbour
trellis above

garage
24'-0" x 27'-0" avg.

motorcourt

covered walkway

studio/ guest
14'-0" x 12'-0"
10'-0" clg.

wetbar

PHOTO ABOVE: *A view across
the 600 square feet of covered
veranda in the rear of the home.*

PLAN | *6748 Grayhawk Trail*

4 Bedroom

5-1/2 Bath

Width: 102'0"

Depth: 131'4"

Exterior Walls: 8" CBS

Living Area: 5,464 sq ft

1st Floor: 4,470 sq ft

2nd Floor: 680 sq ft

Studio/Guest: 314 sq ft

Foundation: Slab

Price Code: **PSE5**

Please note: Home photographed may differ from blueprint.

PLAN | *6733a Rosewood Court*

Photography: Laurence Taylor

PHOTO ABOVE: *Luxury, livability and a love of the outdoors take a Mediterranean turn in this spectacular, contemporary design that revels in a lush tropical landscape. Gardens are everywhere, including the front courtyard, where approaching guests are treated to a majestic recessed entry.*

PHOTO RIGHT: *Four stately tapered columns enclose the octagonal formal dining room. In addition to their meal, guests are served scenic views of the courtyard garden through a set of bay windows.*

PHOTO ABOVE: *Two sets of double doors bookend a grand, picture-perfect arch-top window in this fabulous formal living room. The exquisite ceiling design is an immediate eye-catcher, the only possible distraction is the scenic view your guests will be treated to via expansive glass windows and doors.*

PHOTO LEFT: *The kitchen is equipped to prepare gourmet meals or act as a fun gathering spot for a casual meal or snack. Located alongside the nook and leisure room, the kitchen provides counter-style seating and a food-prep island, as well as plenty of open space for entertaining.*

PHOTO ABOVE: *Rich, dark wood cabinets and moldings make elegant accents, as seen in this private study off the foyer.*

PHOTO ABOVE: *Slender decorative columns and views of the master garden surround this beckoning tub in the master bath.*

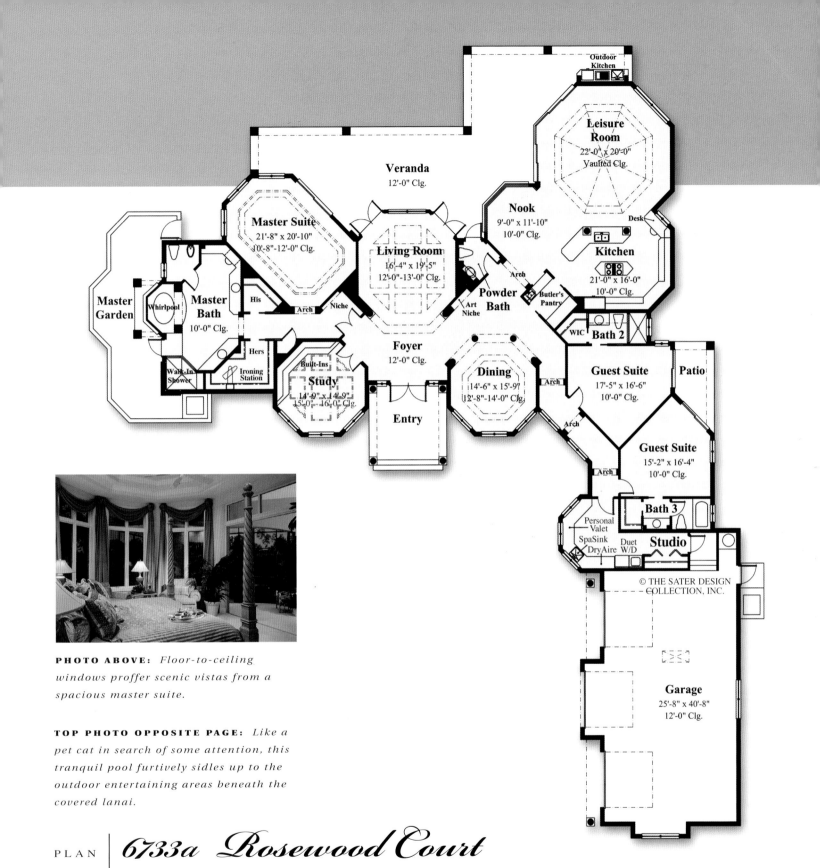

PHOTO ABOVE: *Floor-to-ceiling windows proffer scenic vistas from a spacious master suite.*

TOP PHOTO OPPOSITE PAGE: *Like a pet cat in search of some attention, this tranquil pool furtively sidles up to the outdoor entertaining areas beneath the covered lanai.*

PLAN | *6733a Rosewood Court*

3 Bedroom

3-1/2 Bath

Width: 101'8"

Depth: 128'4"

Exterior Walls: 8" CBS

Living Area: 3,688 sq ft

Foundation: Slab

Price Code: **PSE5**

Includes Whirlpool® Family Studio

Please note: Home photographed may differ from blueprint.

Photography: Oscar Thompson

PHOTO ABOVE: *Nestled in a lush tropical setting, this resort home beautifully blends modern amenities with Mediterranean architectural design tradition. Curved bay windows on either side of the recessed entry provide scenic views from inside the home, as well as an impressive view from the street.*

PHOTO RIGHT: *Bowed glass and a volume ceiling lend an air of spaciousness to the formal dining room that comfortably accommodates up to six guests.*

PHOTO ABOVE: *The lanai offers not only shelter, but ample outdoor entertainment opportunities. Sliding glass doors in both the living and leisure rooms beautifully erase the boundaries between interior and exterior.*

PHOTO LEFT: *Resplendent relaxation is just an armchair away in this grand leisure room, designed to extend out into the lanai via zero-corner sliding glass doors. A wall of built-ins provides plenty of real estate for the latest in multi-media equipment.*

PHOTO ABOVE: *Scenic panoramas are provided by three vertical expanses of glass stretching nearly the full height to the tray ceiling.*

PHOTO ABOVE: *The kitchen — featuring a walk-in pantry, writing desk, generous cabinet storage, double sinks and casual counter seating — is as functional as it is charming.*

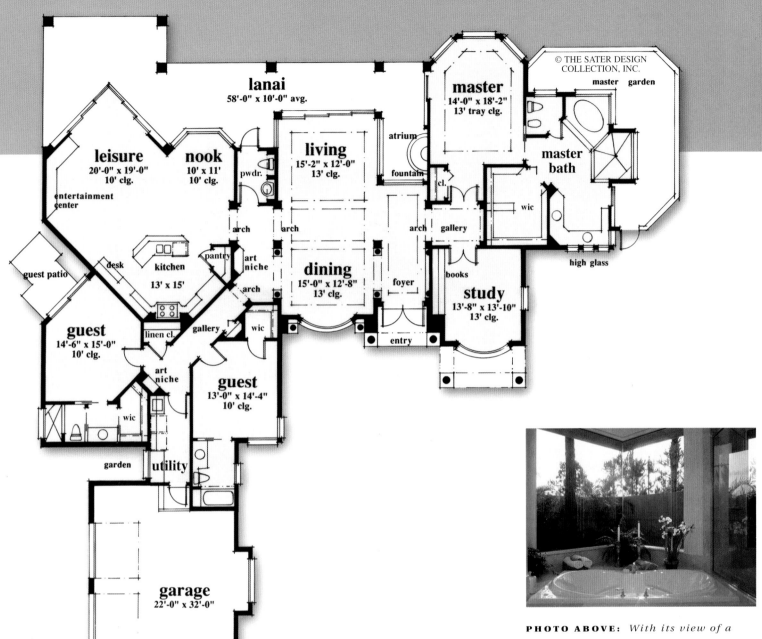

leisure
20'-0" x 19'-0"
10' clg.

nook
10' x 11'
10' clg.

lanai
58'-0" x 10'-0" avg.

living
15'-2" x 12'-0"
13' clg.

atrium

fountain

master
14'-0" x 18'-2"
13' tray clg.

master garden

© THE SATER DESIGN
COLLECTION, INC.

entertainment
center

pwdr.

master
bath

wic

arch

arch

guest patio

desk

kitchen
13' x 15'

pantry

art
niche

arch

dining
15'-0" x 12'-8"
13' clg.

arch

gallery

cl.

high glass

guest
14'-6" x 15'-0"
10' clg.

linen cl.

gallery

wic

foyer

arch

books

study
13'-8" x 13'-10"
13' clg.

art
niche

entry

guest
13'-0" x 14'-4"
10' clg.

wic

garden

utility

garage
22'-0" x 32'-0"

TOP PHOTO OPPOSITE PAGE:
*Custom-designed for outdoor comfort,
this glorious, covered lanai is
bordered by six grand columns.
Nestled between the living room and
master suite is an atrium, home to a
decorative fountain.*

PHOTO ABOVE: *With its view of a
private garden, walk-in glass shower
and sunken tub, the master bath serves
as a restful retreat.*

PHOTO ABOVE: *Your guests deserve
only the best — this guest suite boasts
its own private patio.*

PLAN | *6657* *Biltmore Trace*

3 Bedroom

3-1/2 Bath

Width: 90'0"

Depth: 105'0"

Exterior Walls: 8" CBS

Living Area: 3,244 sq ft

Foundation: Slab

Price Code: **C4**

Please note: Home photographed may differ from blueprint.

Photography: Oscar Thompson

PHOTO ABOVE: *An extended, sheltered entry creates a grand approach that beckons from the façade of this contemporary resort home — a portent of things to come. Once inside the foyer, guests discover that the combination of open floor plan, graceful arches and volume ceilings creates an interior space that is every bit as grand.*

PHOTO RIGHT: *Four out of five guests surveyed will probably say that the focal point of the formal dining room is its unique buffet server. The fifth would cite the room's equally stylish twelve-foot stepped ceiling.*

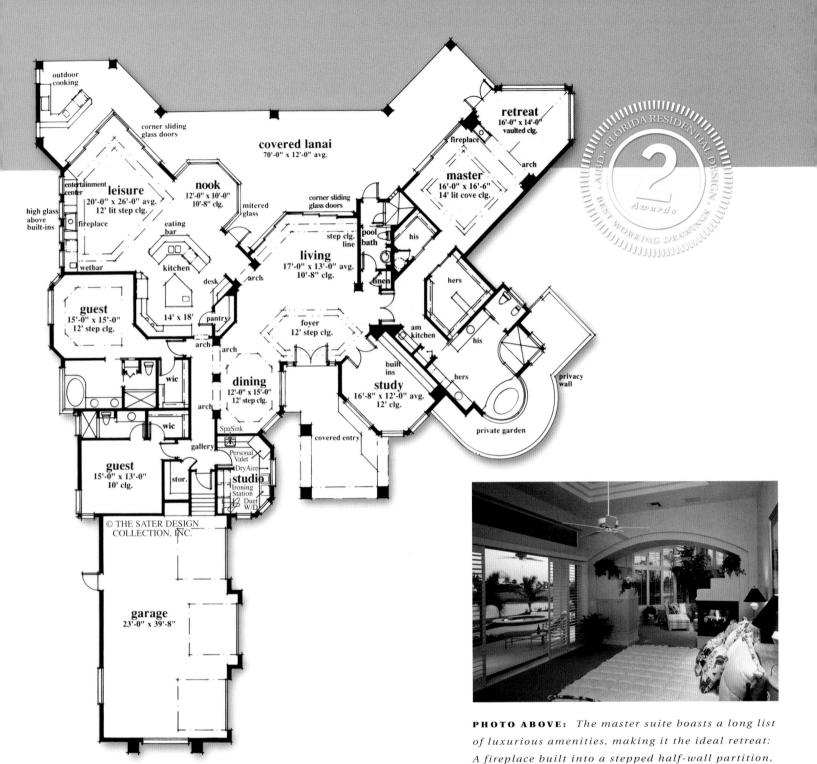

outdoor cooking

corner sliding glass doors

covered lanai
70'-0" x 12'-0" avg.

retreat
16'-0" x 14'-0"
vaulted clg.

fireplace

arch

master
16'-0" x 16'-6"
14' lit cove clg.

entertainment center

leisure
20'-0" x 26'-0" avg.
12' lit step clg.

fireplace

nook
12'-0" x 10'-0"
10'-8" clg.

mitered glass

corner sliding glass doors

step clg. line

pool bath

his

high glass above built-ins

wetbar

eating bar

kitchen

desk

arch

living
17'-0" x 13'-0" avg.
10'-8" clg.

linen

his

hers

guest
15'-0" x 15'-0"
12' step clg.

14' x 18'

pantry

arch

foyer
12' step clg.

am kitchen

his

arch

arch

built ins

study
16'-8" x 12'-0" avg.
12' clg.

hers

privacy wall

wic

dining
12'-0" x 15'-0"
12' step clg.

hers

wic

arch

SpaSink

private garden

guest
15'-0" x 13'-0"
10' clg.

stor.

gallery

Personal Valet

DryAire

studio
Ironing Station
Duet W/D

covered entry

© THE SATER DESIGN COLLECTION, INC.

garage
23'-0" x 39'-8"

PHOTO ABOVE: *The master suite boasts a long list of luxurious amenities, making it the ideal retreat: A fireplace built into a stepped half-wall partition, morning kitchen, spacious sitting area, access to the covered lanai and, finally, a spacious master bath with views of the private garden.*

PLAN | **6670** *Princeville Court*

3 Bedroom

4 Bath

Width: 98'10"

Depth: 126'6"

Exterior Walls: 8" CBS

Living Area: 4,279 sq ft

Foundation: Slab

Price Code: **L2**

Please note: Home photographed may differ from blueprint.
Not available for construction in Lee or Collier Counties, Florida.

PLAN | *6660a Sunningdale Cove*

Photography: Laurence Taylor

PHOTO ABOVE: *This two-story, Mediterranean-style courtyard home is truly unique. What appears to be a stately entry into the home is, in fact, a portico entry that grants access to a spacious courtyard. In this particular design, the courtyard became the perfect spot for a gorgeous pool with spa.*

PHOTO RIGHT: *A second-story observation deck ringed in wrought-iron overlooks a stately turret — home to the study — providing not only panoramic views, but shelter from the elements for the main entrance into the home.*

PHOTO ABOVE: *The serene beauty of the home's design is reflected most perfectly in this view of the courtyard. Anchoring the left side of the pool is the octagonal study, while across the placid water, retreating glass doors open to reveal a generous leisure room.*

PHOTO LEFT: *With a soaring seventeen foot ceiling, two-story bay windows facing the lanai (and with any luck, the ocean), carved coffers and decorative columns, this Grand Room truly lives up to its name in every respect.*

PHOTO ABOVE: *A sculpted arch subtly and elegantly delineates the grand room from the formal dining room. Retreating glass doors and volume ceilings add to the effect.*

PHOTO ABOVE: *Together, the leisure room and breakfast nook offer ample space to relax, converse and enjoy panoramic views of the courtyard through the expanses of glass that border the lanai.*

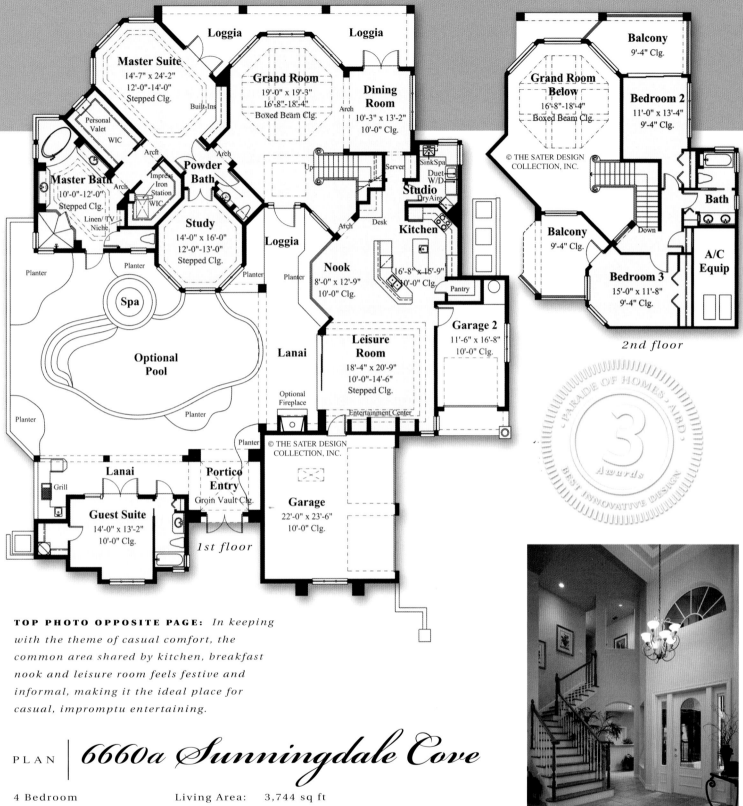

Master Suite
14'-7" x 24'-2"
12'-0"-14'-0"
Stepped Clg.

Loggia

Loggia

Balcony
9'-4" Clg.

Grand Room
19'-0" x 19'-3"
16'-8"-18'-4"
Boxed Beam Clg.

Dining Room
10'-3" x 13'-2"
10'-0" Clg.

Grand Room Below
16'-8"-18'-4"
Boxed Beam Clg.

Bedroom 2
11'-0" x 13'-4"
9'-4" Clg.

© THE SATER DESIGN COLLECTION, INC.

Personal Valet

WIC

Powder Bath

Built-Ins

Arch

Arch

Master Bath
10'-0"-12'-0"
Stepped Clg.

Impress Iron Station

WIC

Linen/TV Niche

Arch

Arch

Study
14'-0" x 16'-0"
12'-0"-13'-0"
Stepped Clg.

Up

Server

Sink Spa

Duet W/D

Studio

DryAire

Desk

Kitchen
16'-8" x 15'-9"
10'-0" Clg.

Arch

Bath

Down

Balcony
9'-4" Clg.

Bedroom 3
15'-0" x 11'-8"
9'-4" Clg.

A/C Equip

Planter

Planter

Planter

Loggia

Planter

Planter

Nook
8'-0" x 12'-9"
10'-0" Clg.

Pantry

2nd floor

Spa

Optional Pool

Lanai

Leisure Room
18'-4" x 20'-9"
10'-0"-14'-6"
Stepped Clg.

Optional Fireplace

Garage 2
11'-6" x 16'-8"
10'-0" Clg.

Planter

Planter

Entertainment Center

Planter

© THE SATER DESIGN COLLECTION, INC.

Lanai

Grill

Guest Suite
14'-0" x 13'-2"
10'-0" Clg.

Portico Entry
Groin Vault Clg.

Garage
22'-0" x 23'-6"
10'-0" Clg.

1st floor

TOP PHOTO OPPOSITE PAGE: *In keeping with the theme of casual comfort, the common area shared by kitchen, breakfast nook and leisure room feels festive and informal, making it the ideal place for casual, impromptu entertaining.*

PLAN | *6660a Sunningdale Cove*

4 Bedroom	Living Area: 3,744 sq ft
3-1/2 Bath	1st Floor: 2,822 sq ft
Width: 80'0"	2nd Floor: 610 sq ft
Depth: 96'0"	Guest House: 312 sq ft
Exterior Walls:	Foundation: Slab
8" CBS or 2x6	Price Code: **L2**

Includes Whirlpool® Family Studio

PHOTO ABOVE: *The home's second story features two additional bedrooms, each with its own private observation deck and accessible by a staircase to the right of the entry.*

Please note: Home photographed may differ from blueprint.

PLAN | *6641a Broadmoor Walk*

Photography: Oscar Thompson

PHOTO ABOVE: *Stately columns support a lovely arched entry with a dramatic bayed turret by its side. This attractive, contemporary-style villa stretches out beneath a turquoise sky. Its interior invites the outside in via a myriad of windows and doors — five sets of double doors, in fact.*

PHOTO RIGHT: *Mirrored in a tranquil pool, this spectacular covered lanai — its graceful arches and statuesque column design inspired by the vernacular made famous by ancient Rome villas — brings an unparalleled opulence to outdoor entertaining. Three sets of elegant French doors provide access from the common area shared by the living and dining rooms.*

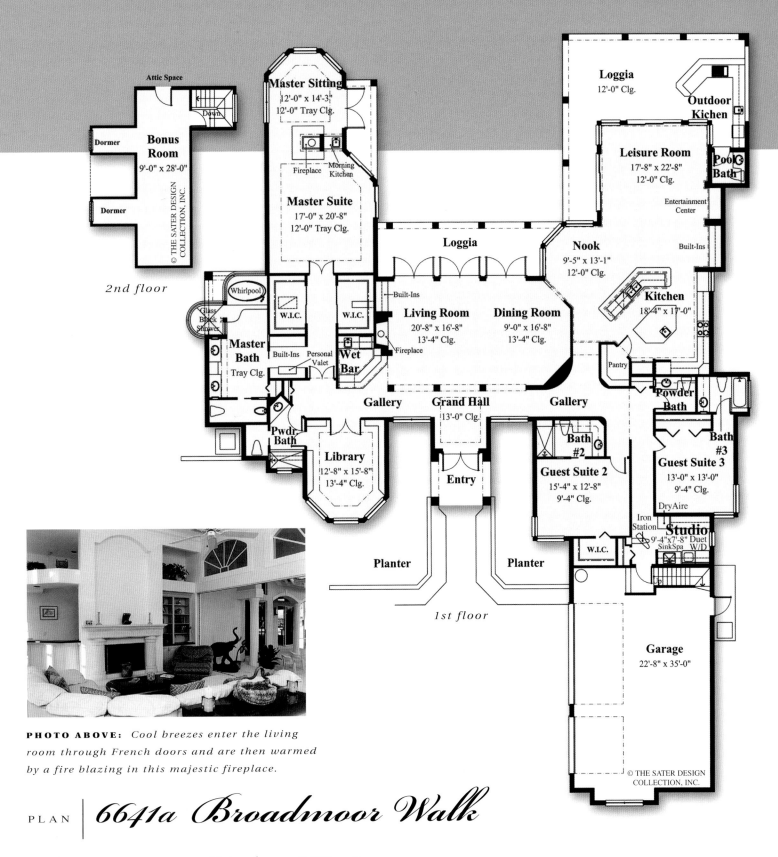

Attic Space

Bonus Room
9'-0" x 28'-0"

Down

Dormer

Dormer

© THE SATER DESIGN COLLECTION, INC.

2nd floor

Master Sitting
12'-0" x 14'-3"
12'-0" Tray Clg.

Fireplace

Morning Kitchen

Master Suite
17'-0" x 20'-8"
12'-0" Tray Clg.

Whirlpool

Glass Block Shower

Master Bath
Tray Clg.

W.I.C.

Built-Ins

Personal Valet

W.I.C.

Wet Bar

Built-Ins

Fireplace

Loggia

Living Room
20'-8" x 16'-8"
13'-4" Clg.

Dining Room
9'-0" x 16'-8"
13'-4" Clg.

Nook
9'-5" x 13'-1"
12'-0" Clg.

Loggia
12'-0" Clg.

Outdoor Kichen

Pool Bath

Leisure Room
17'-8" x 22'-8"
12'-0" Clg.

Entertainment Center

Built-Ins

Kitchen
18'-4" x 17'-0"

Pantry

Pwdr. Bath

Gallery

Grand Hall
13'-0" Clg.

Gallery

Powder Bath

Library
12'-8" x 15'-8"
13'-4" Clg.

Entry

Bath #2

Guest Suite 2
15'-4" x 12'-8"
9'-4" Clg.

W.I.C.

Bath #3

Guest Suite 3
13'-0" x 13'-0"
9'-4" Clg.

DryAire

Iron Station

Studio
9'-4"x7'-8" Duet W/D
SinkSpa

Planter

Planter

1st floor

Garage
22'-8" x 35'-0"

© THE SATER DESIGN COLLECTION, INC.

PHOTO ABOVE: *Cool breezes enter the living room through French doors and are then warmed by a fire blazing in this majestic fireplace.*

PLAN | *6641a Broadmoor Walk*

3 Bedroom

4 Full & 2 Half Baths

Width: 90'0"

Depth: 128'8"

Exterior Walls: 8"CBS or 2x6

Living Area: 3,896 sq ft

1st Floor: 3,896 sq ft

Bonus Room: 356 sq ft

Foundation: Slab

Price Code: **L1**

Includes Whirlpool® Family Studio

Please note: Home photographed may differ from blueprint.

PLAN | *6636a Grand Cypress Lane*

Photography: Oscar Thompson

PHOTO ABOVE: *A deeply recessed entry gives this contemporary villa its grand countenance. Every design element — from gable roof and vaulted ceiling to graceful arch and stately columns — is a celebration of open space, and contributes to the majestic height and breadth that is evident from façade to rear elevation.*

PHOTO RIGHT: *The rear elevation of the home is as impressive as its front. The magnificent decorative arch and column theme of the recessed entry is carried through to the rear by a gable roof.*

PHOTO ABOVE: *What a combination of features: A uniquely elegant corner fireplace, bay-windowed sitting room with convenient morning kitchen, retreating sliding glass doors that open onto the lanai and soaring fourteen-foot ceiling. This isn't just a master suite — it's a masterpiece.*

PHOTO LEFT: *Sunlight streams into the informal areas of the home through broad expanses of glass facing the lanai. Kitchen, nook and leisure room blend together to create a family area that is bright and cheery, open and extremely functional.*

PHOTO ABOVE: *The scenic panoramas visible from inside the home almost pale in comparison to this view of the home itself from outside the rear elevation. Two pairs of stately Tuscan columns on pedestals stoically support a majestic gable overlooking the lanai. Paneled windows stretch skyward, complementing the vaulted ceiling of the formal living room. Meanwhile, to the right, an outdoor kitchen with counter-style seating offers the option of casual dining poolside.*

PHOTO RIGHT: *The unique, "U-shaped" design of this gourmet kitchen provides convenient access to both the breakfast nook on one end and the dining room on the other — not to mention, easy movement between refrigerator, range, cook-top and sinks.*

150 DAN SATER'S LUXURY HOME PLANS

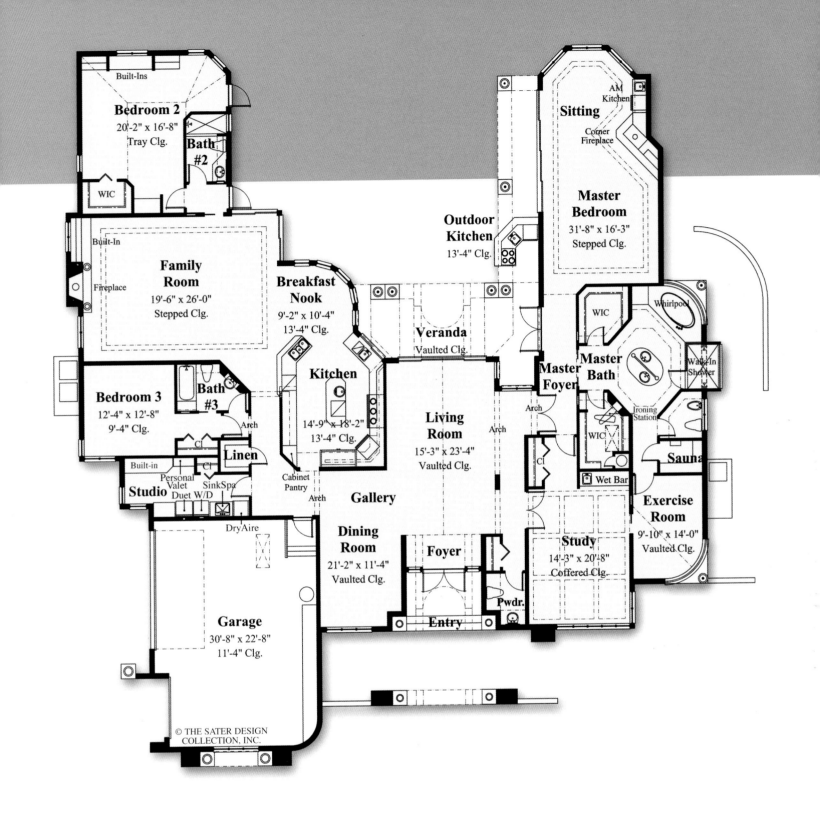

Built-Ins

Bedroom 2
20'-2" x 16'-8"
Tray Clg.

Bath #2

WIC

Built-In

Fireplace

Family Room
19'-6" x 26'-0"
Stepped Clg.

Breakfast Nook
9'-2" x 10'-4"
13'-4" Clg.

Outdoor Kitchen
13'-4" Clg.

AM Kitchen

Sitting

Corner Fireplace

Master Bedroom
31'-8" x 16'-3"
Stepped Clg.

Whirlpool

WIC

Kitchen
14'-9" x 18'-2"
13'-4" Clg.

Veranda
Vaulted Clg.

Master Foyer

Arch

Master Bath

Walk-In Shower

Bedroom 3
12'-4" x 12'-8"
9'-4" Clg.

Bath #3

Arch

Linen

Cl

Built-in

Cl

Personal Valet

SinkSpa

Studio

Duet W/D

Cabinet Pantry

Living Room
15'-3" x 23'-4"
Vaulted Clg.

Arch

Arch

Ironing Station

WIC

Wet Bar

Sauna

Gallery

Arch

Exercise Room
9'-10" x 14'-0"
Vaulted Clg.

DryAire

Dining Room
21'-2" x 11'-4"
Vaulted Clg.

Foyer

Study
14'-3" x 20'-8"
Coffered Clg.

Pwdr.

Garage
30'-8" x 22'-8"
11'-4" Clg.

Entry

© THE SATER DESIGN COLLECTION, INC.

PLAN | *6636a Grand Cypress Lane*

3 Bedroom

3-1/2 Baths

Width: 88'0"

Depth: 95'0"

Exterior Walls: 8" CBS

Living Area: 4,565 sq ft

Foundation: Slab

Price Code: **L2**

Includes Whirlpool® Family Studio

Please note: Home photographed may differ from blueprint.

PLAN | *6944a Maxina*

Photography: Laurence Taylor

PHOTO ABOVE: *It was Andrea Palladio who, over four-hundred fifty years ago, conceived of adapting the pediment and columns of Greek architecture to private residences. The grand portico entry and elaborately decorative balustrades of this lovely Mediterranean are classic examples of the indelible mark the Greek and Romans have made on modern architectural design.*

PHOTO RIGHT: *Guests seated at this formal dining room table are treated to a view of the night sky through this splendid arch-top window.*

PHOTO FAR RIGHT: *Elegant in its simplicity, this understated study can provide much-needed sanctuary at the end of a hectic day. All that's required is a refreshing drink and a favorite book.*

PHOTO ABOVE: *This leisure room, with its beautifully crafted built-ins and stepped ceiling, is almost too grand for "lounging around." Almost, but not quite, thanks to a couple of well-placed, overstuffed chairs.*

PHOTO RIGHT: *The melding of contemporary convenience and classical architectural influences are reflected in the rear elevation, where interior light spills onto decorative columns through sliding glass doors.*

PHOTO ABOVE: *The "common zone" created by the nook, kitchen and leisure room provides ample entertaining space, all but eliminating the question everyone seems to ask when having guests: "Where should we sit?"*

PHOTO LEFT: *A true "space saver," this kitchen is highly efficient. Every inch of space is put to good use, making the chef's job as easy as it can be. All that's left is the clean up.*

FAMILY STUDIO RIGHT:
*When is a laundry room
more than just a laundry
room? When it's a
Whirlpool® Family Studio.
A totally new concept in
home planning, the
Family Studio is a place
designed to make every day
more productive as you
clean and care for all
your clothes.*

BOTTOM LEFT PHOTO:
*The Duet® Fabric-Care
System and Personal Valet.*

PHOTO ABOVE: *The Impress™ Ironing
Station and DryAire™ Drying Cabinet.*

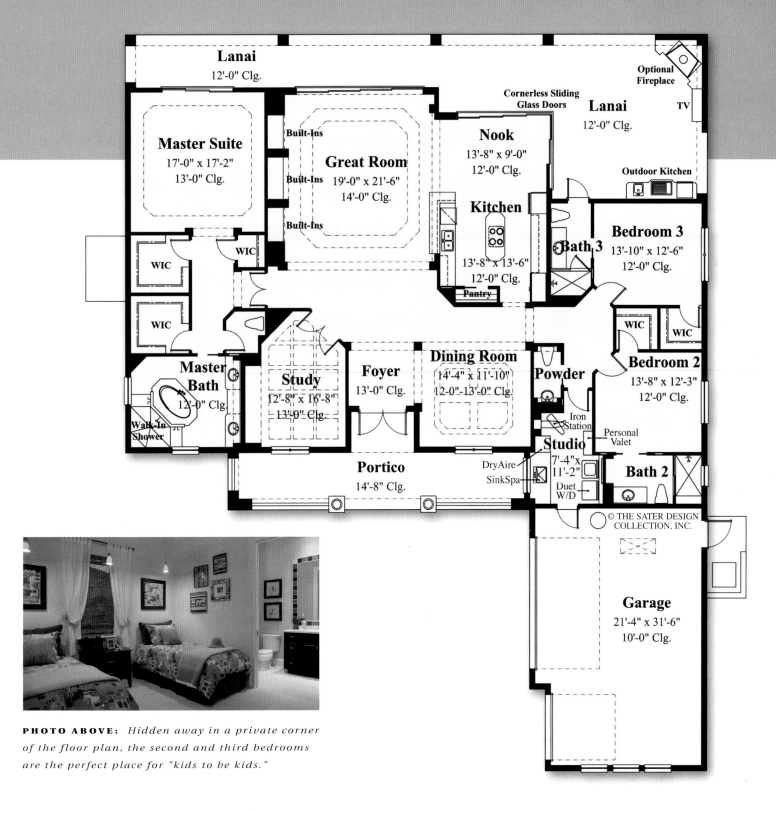

Lanai
12'-0" Clg.

Master Suite
17'-0" x 17'-2"
13'-0" Clg.

Built-Ins

Great Room
19'-0" x 21'-6"
14'-0" Clg.

Built-Ins

Built-Ins

WIC

WIC

WIC

Master
Bath
12'-0" Clg.

Walk-In
Shower

Study
12'-8" x 16'-8"
13'-0" Clg.

Foyer
13'-0" Clg.

Optional
Fireplace

TV

Cornerless Sliding
Glass Doors

Lanai
12'-0" Clg.

Nook
13'-8" x 9'-0"
12'-0" Clg.

Kitchen
13'-8" x 13'-6"
12'-0" Clg.

Outdoor Kitchen

Bath 3

Bedroom 3
13'-10" x 12'-6"
12'-0" Clg.

Pantry

WIC

WIC

Dining Room
14'-4" x 11'-10"
12'-0"-13'-0" Clg.

Powder

Bedroom 2
13'-8" x 12'-3"
12'-0" Clg.

Iron
Station

Personal
Valet

Studio
7'-4" x
11'-2"

DryAire

SinkSpa

Duet
W/D

Bath 2

Portico
14'-8" Clg.

© THE SATER DESIGN
COLLECTION, INC.

Garage
21'-4" x 31'-6"
10'-0" Clg.

PHOTO ABOVE: *Hidden away in a private corner of the floor plan, the second and third bedrooms are the perfect place for "kids to be kids."*

PLAN | *6944a Maxina*

3 Bedroom

3-1/2 Bath

Width: 74'0"

Depth: 90'2"

Exterior Walls: 8" CBS

Living Area: 3,104 sq ft

Foundation: Slab

Price Code: **PSE5**

Includes Whirlpool® Family Studio

TOP PHOTO OPPOSITE PAGE: *The center-piece of this casual gathering place, the covered lanai, is also one of the hottest items in outdoor entertaining today — the KitchenAid® outdoor grill. Dining al fresco never tasted better!*

Please note: Home photographed may differ from blueprint.
Not available for construction in Lee or Collier Counties, Florida.

Photography: Doug Thompson

PHOTO ABOVE: *The charming entry portico of this contemporary cottage creates an idyllic scene at sunset. Warm breezes weave their way between the rustic columns of stacked stone and shapely balusters, and then, into windows half-open. Meanwhile, the last vestiges of sunlight give the home's tile roof a red-purple glow.*

PHOTO RIGHT: *Here, the kitchen is viewed from the great room. Evocative of a simpler time, this elegant, down-to-earth design defines homey comfort while offering the chef of the house the latest in conveniences.*

PHOTO ABOVE: *A massive stone hearth takes an authoritative position in the corner of this casual living zone, created by the melding of kitchen, nook and covered lanai.*

PHOTO LEFT: *A panoramic view of the landscape stretches from one end of the great room to the other, like a billboard painted with twilight outdoor scenery.*

PHOTO ABOVE: *The great room takes on even greater proportions as it transitions effortlessly into the kitchen, nook and, ultimately, the lanai.*

PHOTO RIGHT: *Just off the foyer, the study is a great space for a home office. Of course, if you do enough work outside the home, it's a great place to just rest and relax, too.*

PHOTO FAR RIGHT: *Ordinarily, ceilings are not a topic of conversation at dinner parties. They very well could be here, however, given the beautifully crafted, stepped ceiling in the dining room.*

PHOTO ABOVE: *The entire left side of the home is dedicated to a spacious master suite. Here, a comfy garden tub shares a partial wall with the walk-in shower for two on the opposite side.*

PHOTO ABOVE: *The retreating glass doors of the master suite add dramatic views of the exterior landscape beyond the covered lanai.*

Verandah 10'-0" Clg

Outdoor Fireplace

Master Suite 13'-0" x 16'-10" 10'-0" - 10'-8" Stepped Clg.

Built-Ins

Great Room 19'-4" x 21'-4" Vaulted Clg.

Built-Ins

Built-Ins

Nook 12'-10" x 6'-10" 10'-0" Clg.

Grille

Guest Suite 2 13'-10" x 12'-6" 10'-0" Clg.

Kitchen 12'-10" x 13'-6" 10'-0" Clg.

WIC

WIC

Master Foyer

Bath 2

Linen

WIC WIC

Master Bath 10'-0" Clg.

Make-Up Area

Study 11'-2" x 16'-9" 12'-0" - 12'-8" Beamed Clg.

Foyer 12'-0" Clg.

Desk

Seat

Guest Suite 1 13'-8" x 12'-3" 10'-0" Clg.

Dining 13'-10" x 12'-10" 12'-0" - 13'-0" Stepped Clg.

Built-Ins

Entry

Utility 7'-4" x 10'-9"

Bath 1

Garage 21'-4" x 21'-6" 10'-0" Clg.

© THE SATER DESIGN COLLECTION, INC.

TOP PHOTO OPPOSITE PAGE: *An outdoor kitchen and sitting area (to left) are easily accessible from every room in the rear elevation via sliding glass doors, most notably the great room and breakfast nook.*

PLAN | *6780* *Hammock Grove*

3 Bedroom

3 Bath

Width: 72'0"

Depth: 80'0"

Exterior Walls: 2x6 or 8" CBS

Living Area: 2,885 sq ft

Foundation: Slab

Price Code: **PSE5**

Please note: Home photographed may differ from blueprint. Not available for construction in Lee or Collier Counties, Florida.

PLAN | *6945a San Sebastian*

Photography: Laurence Taylor

PHOTO ABOVE: *The influence of the Spanish vernacular is abundantly evident in this remarkable Mediterranean-style villa. With a quixotic loftiness evocative of Spanish missions — tile roof, textured stucco, decorative brackets and an arched recess entry that recalls a bell tower — this noble home both looks, and feels, like a sanctuary — a place where one's privacy and comfort are truly sacred.*

PHOTO RIGHT: *This intimate dining room, nestled in the front of the floor plan just off the foyer, serves as a lavish setting for a formal dinner party.*

PHOTO ABOVE: *Arches, columns and stepped ceilings create a cathedral-like serenity throughout the entire interior, including this formal living area.*

PHOTO LEFT: *The entire left side of the home is dedicated to an opulent, sequestered master suite that encompasses several rooms, including a view-oriented sitting area and spacious master bath.*

PHOTO ABOVE: *Leisure room and breakfast nook are conjoined to create an informal and highly functional common zone. Zero-corner sliding glass doors add yet another dimension by stylishly incorporating the exterior landscape.*

PHOTO RIGHT: *The ideal evening entertainment venue, the covered lanai is a stellar place for enjoying a night sky or a midnight snack in the outdoor kitchen (far left).*

PHOTO ABOVE: *Arched coffers serve as elegant art niches, bookending a charming fireplace that will warm gatherings in this view-oriented living room.*

FAMILY STUDIO: *Want to really put a laundry room to work? Try the Whirpool® Family Studio. A totally new concept in home planning, the Family Studio is a place designed to make every day more productive as you clean and care for all your clothes. Above, the ImPress™ Ironing Station, Personal Valet®, SinkSpa™ and Duet® Washer and Dryer.*

PHOTO ABOVE: *Pictured above are the SinkSpa™, Duet® Fabric-Care System and the DryAire™ Drying Cabinet.*

Guest Suite
12'-10" x 12'-6"
10'-4" Clg.

Guest Bath

WIC

WIC

Arch

Leisure Room
18'-0" x 22'-8"
Stepped Clg.

Nook
8'-0" x 11'-6"
10'-4" Clg.

Lanai
10'-4" Clg.

Grill

Kitchen
15'-4" x 16'-4"
Stepped Clg.

Arch

Living Room
16'-8" x 15'-6"
Stepped Clg.

Built-Ins

Pwdr Bath

Fireplace

Built-Ins

Master Suite
13'-6" x 18'-4"
Stepped Clg.

Arch

Bedroom 2
12'-10" x 12'-8"
10'-4" Clg.

Pantry

Bath

Arch

Arch

Foyer
10'-4" Clg.

Arch

Master Foyer

Arch

WIC

St.

Arch

Built-Ins

Bedroom 1
12'-0" x 14'-10"
10'-4" Clg.

Personal Valet

SpaSink

Studio
Duet W/D
Iron Station
DryAire

WIC

Arch

Dining Room
11'-2" x 13'-4"
Stepped Clg.

Arch

Entry
10'-4" Clg.

Study
8'-4" x 10'-10"
10'-4" Clg.

Built-Ins

Master Bath
10'-4" Clg.

Whirlpool

Walk-In Shower

Master Garden

A/C

A/C

Garage
21'-8" x 31'-2"
10'-4" Clg.

© THE SATER DESIGN COLLECTION, INC.

PHOTO ABOVE:
KitchenAid® caters to a chef's highest expectations with appliances that deliver professional quality, durability and simplicity. Pictured here are the KitchenAid® double oven and refrigerator.

PHOTO ABOVE: Rejuvenation of both body and spirit can be found in this whirlpool tub that overlooks the privacy garden.

TOP PHOTO OPPOSITE PAGE:
Ergonomically designed, this gourmet kitchen is ultra-efficient — everything required is well within the chef's reach, including state-of-the-art KitchenAid® appliances.

PLAN | *6945a San Sebastian*

4 Bedroom

3-1/2 Bath

Width: 68'8"

Depth: 93'8"

Exterior Walls: 8" CBS

Living Area: 3,433 sq ft

Foundation: Slab

Price Code: **PSE5**

Includes Whirlpool® Family Studio

Please note: Home photographed may differ from blueprint.

Photography: CJ Walker

PHOTO ABOVE: *The noble families of Rome, like city-dwellers today, understood the need for a "countryside" home — a place where they could converse with friends in an informal setting, commune with nature and rejuvenate their spirits. The "villa" was just such a place, and this Italianate villa home is a classic example. As evidenced in the architectural elements of the home's façade, the Romans may have embraced "country life," but the luxuries of city life were always within easy reach.*

PHOTO RIGHT: *Double doors open onto the portico, revealing shapely balusters and a picture-perfect view of the star-filled night sky.*

PHOTO FAR RIGHT: *Gracefully arched built-ins, like beautiful bookends, complement an arch-top, carved art niche over the mantel of this charming living-room fireplace.*

PHOTO ABOVE: *True to the Roman architect's objective in creating a country home that "rejuvenates the spirit," the rear elevation of this villa does just that.*

PHOTO RIGHT: *Decorative columns flank the service counter of the wet bar, which, along with the butler's pantry, conveniently connects the dining room with the kitchen.*

PHOTO FAR RIGHT: *Like a Renaissance work of art, this formal dining room — with double doors that open onto the portico — gives dinner guests a taste of true elegance.*

PHOTO ABOVE: *If ever there were a reason to simply "lay in bed and look at the ceiling," this is it — this gorgeous, twelve-foot stepped ceiling with recessed lighting is a sight to behold.*

PHOTO RIGHT: *The master bath features a mammoth walk-in shower, step-up garden tub and generous "His" and "Her" walk-in closets.*

PHOTO FAR RIGHT: *State-of-the-art appliances make an understated appearance in the gourmet kitchen, inconspicuously supporting the chef in his or her culinary endeavors.*

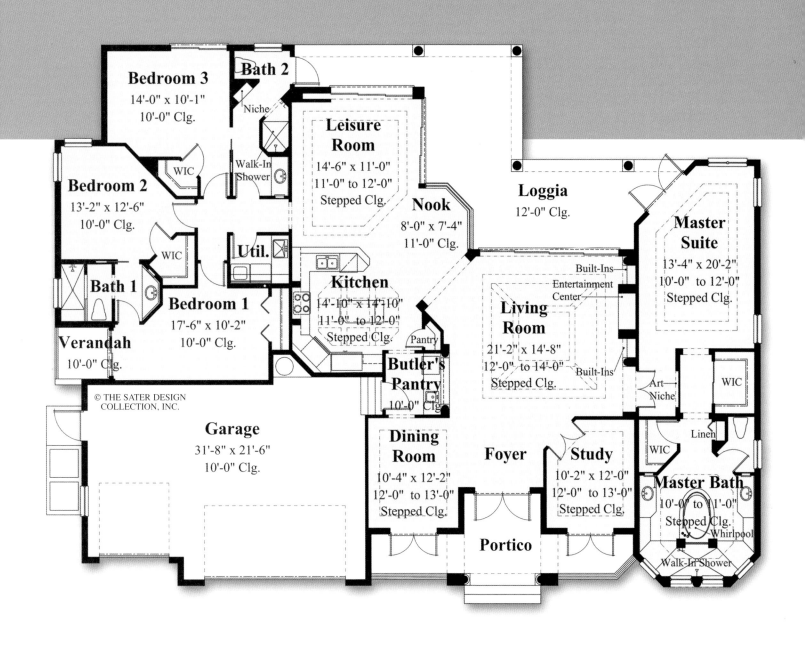

Bedroom 3
14'-0" x 10'-1"
10'-0" Clg.

Bath 2

Niche

Walk-In Shower

WIC

Bedroom 2
13'-2" x 12'-6"
10'-0" Clg.

WIC

Leisure Room
14'-6" x 11'-0"
11'-0" to 12'-0"
Stepped Clg.

Nook
8'-0" x 7'-4"
11'-0" Clg.

Loggia
12'-0" Clg.

Master Suite
13'-4" x 20'-2"
10'-0" to 12'-0"
Stepped Clg.

Built-Ins

Entertainment Center

Bath 1

Util.

Kitchen
14'-10" x 14'-10"
11'-0" to 12'-0"
Stepped Clg.

Bedroom 1
17'-6" x 10'-2"
10'-0" Clg.

Verandah
10'-0" Clg.

Pantry

Living Room
21'-2" x 14'-8"
12'-0" to 14'-0"
Stepped Clg.

Built-Ins

Art Niche

WIC

© THE SATER DESIGN COLLECTION, INC.

Butler's Pantry
10'-0" Clg.

Garage
31'-8" x 21'-6"
10'-0" Clg.

Dining Room
10'-4" x 12'-2"
12'-0" to 13'-0"
Stepped Clg.

Foyer

Study
10'-2" x 12'-0"
12'-0" to 13'-0"
Stepped Clg.

WIC

Linen

Master Bath
10'-0" to 11'-0"
Stepped Clg.

Whirlpool

Walk-In Shower

Portico

PLAN | *6778* | *Deauville*

4 Bedroom

3 Bath

Width: 80'10"

Depth: 59'10"

Exterior Walls: 8" CBS

Living Area: 2,908 sq ft

Foundation: Slab

Price Code: **PSE5**

Please note: Home photographed may differ from blueprint.
Not available for construction in Lee or Collier Counties, Florida.

Photography: Oscar Thompson

PHOTO ABOVE: *Sabal palms line the drive up to this majestic Mediterranean-style villa, a resort home that seems comfortably settled into its natural surroundings. In fact, nature literally goes "as far as the front door." The recessed entry is flanked by two planters, creating a parade of flowers that takes guests right up to the foyer.*

PHOTO RIGHT: *The dark wood of both the built-in cabinets and the exposed-beam ceiling makes this very private study a warm and intimate place to relax with an apéritif or a favorite novel.*

PHOTO ABOVE: *Six, eight-foot-high vertical windows (and on the opposite side of the room, a handsome buffet server) treat dinner guests to a view of the garden area just outside.*

PHOTO ABOVE: *A two-sided corner fireplace warms a well-appointed leisure room — which includes a wet bar and built-in entertainment center.*

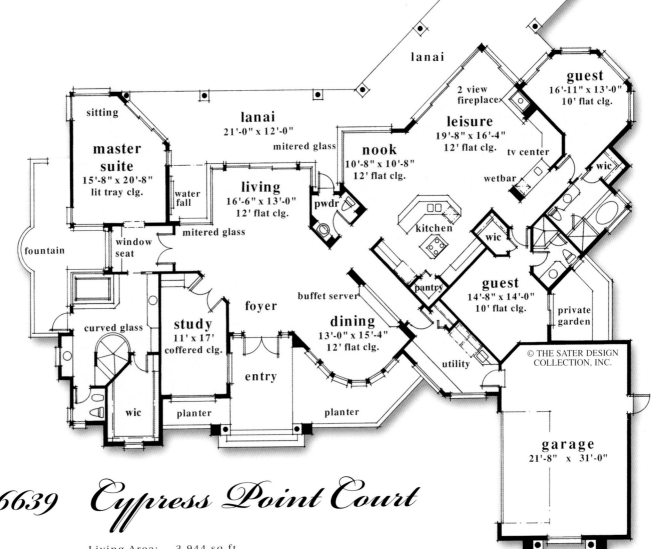

PLAN | *6639* *Cypress Point Court*

3 Bedroom

3-1/2 Bath

Width: 98'0"

Depth: 105'0"

Exterior Walls: 8" CBS

Living Area: 3,944 sq ft

Foundation: Slab

Price Code: **L1**

Please note: Home photographed may differ from blueprint.

Photography: Oscar Thompson

PHOTO ABOVE: *The great Italian architect Palladio felt the home should be a place where one found refreshment and consolation, a respite from agitation. This is as true today in this modern villa as it was in the patrician villas of his day.*

PHOTO RIGHT: *True to Palladio's vision, the rear elevation welcomes in the world outside. In ancient Rome, this was essential for preserving "health, strength and finally, the spirit."*

PHOTO FAR RIGHT: *Corner-pocket sliding glass doors present this spectacular view of the home's interior — the living room and foyer — from the vantage point of the lanai.*

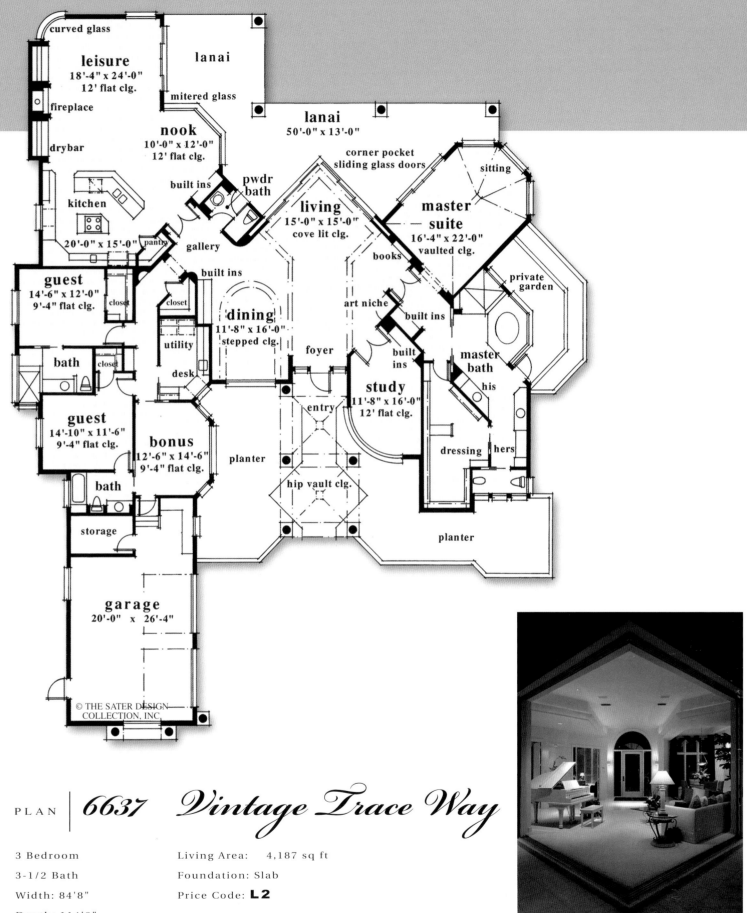

curved glass

leisure
18'-4" x 24'-0"
12' flat clg.

lanai

fireplace

mitered glass

drybar

nook
10'-0" x 12'-0"
12' flat clg.

lanai
50'-0" x 13'-0"

built ins

pwdr
bath

corner pocket
sliding glass doors

sitting

kitchen

20'-0" x 15'-0"

pantry

gallery

living
15'-0" x 15'-0"
cove lit clg.

**master
suite**
16'-4" x 22'-0"
vaulted clg.

books

private
garden

guest
14'-6" x 12'-0"
9'-4" flat clg.

closet

built ins

closet

art niche

built ins

bath

closet

dining
11'-8" x 16'-0"
stepped clg.

utility

desk

foyer

built ins

**master
bath**

his

guest
14'-10" x 11'-6"
9'-4" flat clg.

study
11'-8" x 16'-0"
12' flat clg.

bonus
12'-6" x 14'-6"
9'-4" flat clg.

entry

planter

dressing

hers

bath

hip vault clg.

storage

planter

garage
20'-0" x 26'-4"

© THE SATER DESIGN
COLLECTION, INC.

PLAN | *6637* *Vintage Trace Way*

3 Bedroom

3-1/2 Bath

Width: 84'8"

Depth: 114'0"

Exterior Walls: 8" CBS

Living Area: 4,187 sq ft

Foundation: Slab

Price Code: **L2**

Please note: Home photographed may differ from blueprint.

Photography: Oscar Thompson

PHOTO ABOVE: *A bayed turret and raised entry make a dramatic statement to all who approach. This compact contemporary – three bedrooms, three and one-half baths, a study and a spacious leisure room, all in thirty-five-hundred square feet – would ideally be situated just a short pitch from a favorite golf hole.*

PHOTO RIGHT: *A double-sided fireplace opens on one side to the master suite and on the other to the living room. On the opposite side of the living room is a wet bar, as well as access to the lanai's outdoor grill.*

PHOTO FAR RIGHT: *At twilight, the rear elevation, its myriad windows illuminated from within, sparkles like a small city.*

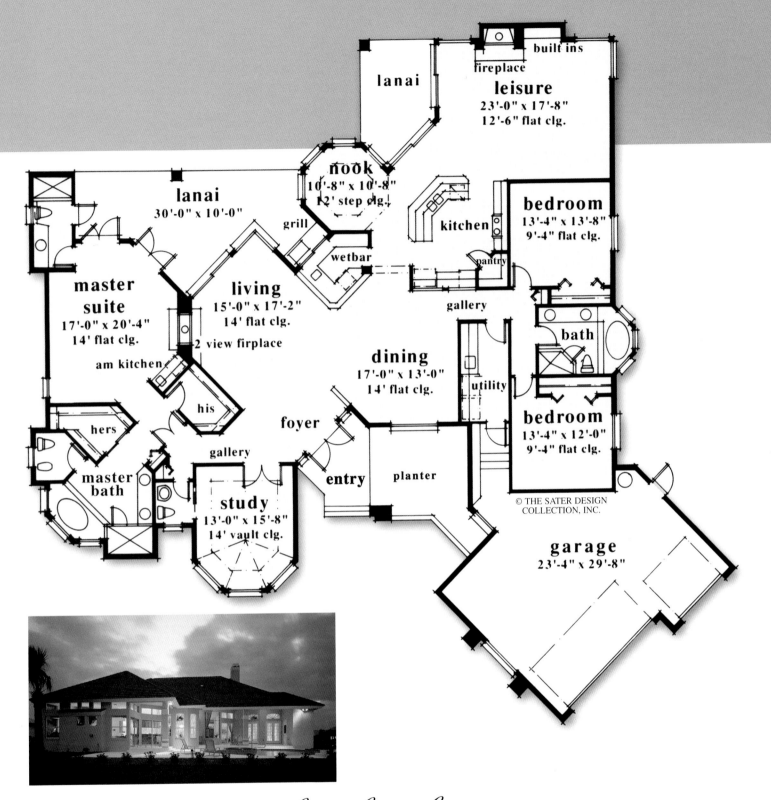

lanai

built ins

fireplace

leisure
23'-0" x 17'-8"
12'-6" flat clg.

nook
10'-8" x 10'-8"
12' step clg.

grill

kitchen

bedroom
13'-4" x 13'-8"
9'-4" flat clg.

lanai
30'-0" x 10'-0"

wetbar

pantry

master
suite
17'-0" x 20'-4"
14' flat clg.

living
15'-0" x 17'-2"
14' flat clg.

gallery

am kitchen

2 view firplace

bath

his

dining
17'-0" x 13'-0"
14' flat clg.

utility

hers

foyer

bedroom
13'-4" x 12'-0"
9'-4" flat clg.

master
bath

gallery

study
13'-0" x 15'-8"
14' vault clg.

entry

planter

© THE SATER DESIGN
COLLECTION, INC.

garage
23'-4" x 29'-8"

PLAN | *6634* *Innsbrook Place*

3 Bedroom

3-1/2 Bath

Width: 95'0"

Depth: 88'8"

Exterior Walls: 8" CBS

Living Area: 3,477 sq ft

Foundation: Slab

Price Code: **C4**

Please note: Home photographed may differ from blueprint.

Photography: Oscar Thompson

PHOTO ABOVE: *Like a warm fire on a cold evening, the recessed entry of this contemporary Mediterranean-style villa beckons to guests with a welcoming glow.*

PHOTO RIGHT: *Zero-corner glass doors penetrate the outdoors at a ninety-degree angle, incorporating the decorative columns and arches of the lanai into the leisure room.*

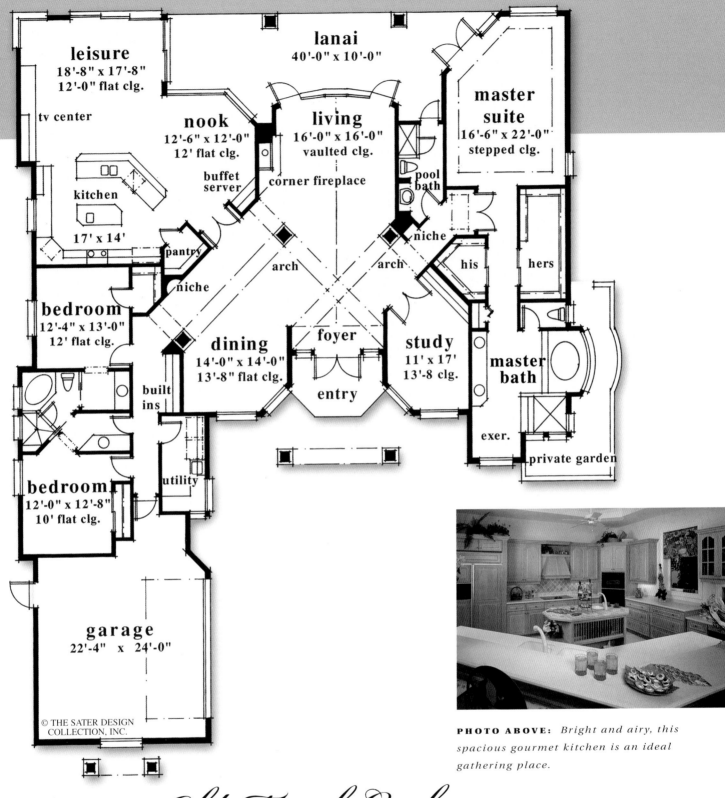

leisure
18'-8" x 17'-8"
12'-0" flat clg.

tv center

lanai
40'-0" x 10'-0"

master suite
16'-6" x 22'-0"
stepped clg.

nook
12'-6" x 12'-0"
12' flat clg.

living
16'-0" x 16'-0"
vaulted clg.

buffet server

corner fireplace

pool bath

kitchen
17' x 14'

pantry

niche

niche

arch

arch

his

hers

bedroom
12'-4" x 13'-0"
12' flat clg.

dining
14'-0" x 14'-0"
13'-8" flat clg.

foyer

study
11' x 17'
13'-8 clg.

master bath

built ins

entry

exer.

bedroom
12'-0" x 12'-8"
10' flat clg.

utility

private garden

garage
22'-4" x 24'-0"

© THE SATER DESIGN
COLLECTION, INC.

PHOTO ABOVE: *Bright and airy, this spacious gourmet kitchen is an ideal gathering place.*

PLAN | *6642* *Old Marsh Circle*

3 Bedroom

3 Bath

Width: 77'0"

Depth: 94'4"

Exterior Walls: 8" CBS

Living Area: 3,743 sq ft

Foundation: Slab

Price Code: **L1**

Please note: Home photographed may differ from blueprint.

Photography: Oscar Thompson

PHOTO ABOVE: *Contemporary and classic design are combined with stellar results in this gracious resort home. Decorative columns and a double-arched entryway speak to a heritage that dates back several hundred years, while contemporary lines and sun-drenched stucco give the home a modern feel and a bright, sunny disposition. Every home has a personality — this one just loves a tropical setting, as you can tell.*

PHOTO RIGHT: *"Bright and sunny" describes much of the interior of the home as well. Here, natural light streams in through a unique bow window in the study, creating inviting warmth and comfort.*

PHOTO ABOVE: *Bathed in sunshine, the rear elevation boasts a spacious covered verandah of nearly six-hundred square feet. There's an outdoor kitchen conveniently tucked away in a shady corner, which means there's practically no reason to go back inside once you're out.*

PHOTO LEFT: *The formal living room is a "white-on-white" work of art. Double doors, opening to the verandah, bring the space both natural light and a touch of simple elegance.*

PHOTO ABOVE: *A unique buffet serves as buffer between the formal dining and living rooms, separating the two spaces and, at the same time, keeping them open and airy.*

PHOTO RIGHT: *Here, a charming fireplace, bookended by built-ins, warms the common area consisting of leisure room, kitchen and breakfast nook.*

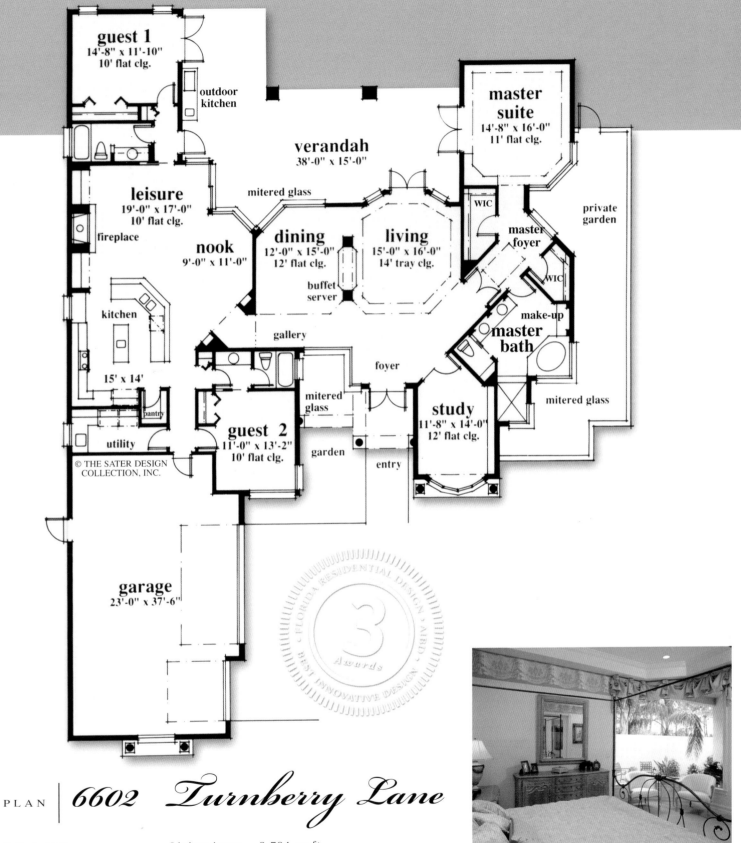

guest 1
14'-8" x 11'-10"
10' flat clg.

outdoor kitchen

verandah
38'-0" x 15'-0"

master suite
14'-8" x 16'-0"
11' flat clg.

leisure
19'-0" x 17'-0"
10' flat clg.

mitered glass

private garden

WIC

fireplace

nook
9'-0" x 11'-0"

dining
12'-0" x 15'-0"
12' flat clg.

living
15'-0" x 16'-0"
14' tray clg.

master foyer

WIC

buffet server

make-up

kitchen

master bath

gallery

15' x 14'

pantry

guest 2
11'-0" x 13'-2"
10' flat clg.

mitered glass

foyer

study
11'-8" x 14'-0"
12' flat clg.

utility

© THE SATER DESIGN
COLLECTION, INC.

garden

mitered glass

entry

garage
23'-0" x 37'-6"

FLORIDA RESIDENTIAL DESIGN • ARID •
3 Awards
BEST INNOVATIVE DESIGN

PLAN | *6602* *Turnberry Lane*

3 Bedroom

3 Bath

Width: 70'0"

Depth: 98'0"

Exterior Walls: 2x6 or 8"CBS

Living Area: 2,794 sq ft

Foundation: Slab

Price Code: **C4**

PHOTO ABOVE: *Calming views of the private garden surround this spacious master suite.*

Please note: Home photographed may differ from blueprint.

PLAN | *6751a Windsor Court*

Photography: Laurence Taylor, Oscar Thompson

PHOTO ABOVE: *Au•da•cious adj: bold, daring or fearless, especially in challenging assumptions or conventions. There is no single word that better describes this palatial and dramatically contemporary residence. Its façade, as impressive as it is, belies the expansive, "paradise on earth" that stretches out from behind its regal courtyard entry.*

PHOTO RIGHT: *The breakfast nook's floor-to-ceiling wall of angled glass provides panoramic, "big-screen" views — views that seem to extend for miles and miles — with the morning's first cup of coffee.*

PHOTO ABOVE: *Winding its way through the property like a lazy river navigating a jungle landscape, the pool proffers blue-water views from several rooms in the home, including the master suite and study.*

PHOTO LEFT: *Tucked away in a private corner and surrounded by lush vegetation, the sun deck is a tranquil retreat. The only sound to be heard is from the nearby waterfall, as water gently cascades into the pool.*

PHOTO ABOVE: *The gathering room, located in the rear of the plan between the master suite and the leisure room, is just that — a great place to gather. There's no better view, nor is there a more convenient place to have a drink, since the room also features a private bar.*

PHOTO RIGHT: *Spacious and lavishly appointed, the master suite is nearly a home unto itself. Up the stairs is an intimate retreat that provides access to the sun deck on one side and private patio on the other.*

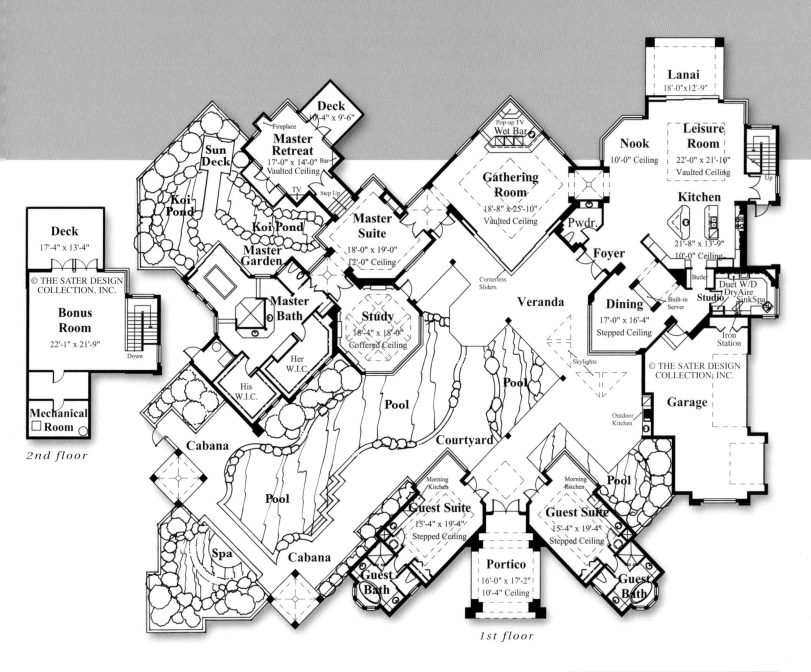

Deck
10'-4" x 9'-6"

Fireplace

Master Retreat
17'-0" x 14'-0"
Vaulted Ceiling

Bar

TV

Step Up

Sun Deck

Koi Pond

Koi Pond

Master Garden

Master Suite
18'-0" x 19'-0"
12'-0" Ceiling

Master Bath

Her W.I.C.

His W.I.C.

Study
18'-4" x 18'-0"
Coffered Ceiling

Pop-up TV
Wet Bar

Gathering Room
18'-8" x 25'-10"
Vaulted Ceiling

Cornerless Sliders

Pwdr.

Foyer

Nook
10'-0" Ceiling

Lanai
18'-0"x 12'-9"

Leisure Room
22'-0" x 21'-10"
Vaulted Ceiling

Kitchen
21'-8" x 13'-9"
10'-0" Ceiling

Up

Butler

Studio

Duet W/D
DryAire
SinkSpa

Veranda

Dining
17'-0" x 16'-4"
Stepped Ceiling

Built-in Server

Iron Station

© THE SATER DESIGN COLLECTION, INC.

Skylights

Pool

Outdoor Kitchen

Garage

Courtyard

Cabana

Pool

Spa

Cabana

Morning Kitchen

Guest Suite
15'-4" x 19'-4"
Stepped Ceiling

Guest Bath

Portico
16'-0" x 17'-2"
10'-4" Ceiling

Morning Kitchen

Pool

Guest Suite
15'-4" x 19'-4"
Stepped Ceiling

Guest Bath

1st floor

Deck
17'-4" x 13'-4"

© THE SATER DESIGN COLLECTION, INC.

Bonus Room
22'-1" x 21'-9"

Down

Mechanical Room

2nd floor

PLAN | *6751a Windsor Court*

3 Bedroom

3-1/2 Bath

Width: 137'4"

Depth: 103'0"

Exterior Walls: 8" CBS

Living Area: 6,457 sq ft

1st Floor: 4,715 sq ft

2nd Floor: 570 sq ft

Bonus Room: 1,172 sq ft

Foundation: Slab

Price Code: **PSE5**

Includes Whirlpool® Family Studio

Please note: Home photographed may differ from blueprint.

PHOTO ABOVE: *This spectacular study seems to hover above the ground, while offering a one-hundred-eighty-degree view of the world outside.*

PLAN | *6750a The Cardiff*

Photography: Oscar Thompson

PHOTO ABOVE: *This majestic Mediterranean proudly displays its Revival roots. An elegant gabled entry, tapered columns and octagonal turrets are all inspired by original Italian villas and contribute to the classic and timeless beauty of this design. Rose-pink barrel tile and natural-toned stucco give the villa a sense of earthiness.*

PHOTO RIGHT: *The home's octagonal study, with a thirteen-foot tray ceiling, is intimate yet cheerful — four of the eight sides are glass, offering plenty of sunlight and scenery.*

PHOTO ABOVE: Like "the big screen" at a movie theater, open sliding glass doors in the living room present the lanai at dusk, a picture-perfect scene to replace what — in most homes — would have been just an ordinary wall.

PHOTO LEFT: The leisure room — with carved nook designed to accommodate an entertainment center — transitions seamlessly through open glass sliding doors to an outdoor kitchen, tucked in a corner of the wraparound lanai.

PHOTO ABOVE: *A plethora of outdoor activities are available at the rear of the home — from swimming and sunning to a game of backgammon in the shade of the covered lanai.*

PHOTO RIGHT: *Open and airy thanks to glass walls and volume ceilings, the area shared by the kitchen, breakfast nook and leisure room takes the idea of "hangout" to new heights.*

© THE SATER DESIGN COLLECTION, INC.

Lanai
12' 0" Flat Ceiling

Outdoor Kitchen
Gas Grill
Bar Sink
Underctr Refrig.

Leisure Room
20' 0" x 17' 0"
11' 4"h. Stepped Ceiling

Entertainment Center Nook

Lanai
12' 0"h. Flat Ceiling

Nook
10' 0" x 10' 0" Avg.
11' 4" Double Stepped Ceiling

Master Suite
21' 6" x 14' 9" Avg.
11' 4"h. Stepped Ceiling

Guest Suite 2
13' 4" x 14' 4"
10' 0"h. Flat Ceiling

42"h. Counter

Kitchen
16' 0" x 16' 0" Avg.
10' 0"h. Ceiling

DW   Dbl. Sink

Desk

Open Shelves

Powder
10' 0" Flat Ceiling Ped Lav

WC

Living Room
16' 0" x 14' 0"
12' 0"h. Flat Ceiling

W.I.C

WC

Lav
Mir
Lav

Master Bath
10' 0" Flat Ceiling

20" h. Deck

Tub

Ledge

10' 0"h. Ceiling

Guest Bath 2
20"h. Tub Deck
Tub
WC   Lav
Mir
Linen Closet

Oven/Micro

Refrig

Cooktop w/Hood

Make Up Table

Seat
Walk In Shower

18" h. Shower Seat
Linen/WC Cab't
Shower
Guest Bath 1

W.I.C.

Pantry

Built-In Server

10' 0" Flat Ceiling

Foyer

Study
14' 0" x 15' 0" Avg.
13' 4"h. Stepped Ceiling

W.I.C
10' 0" Flat Ceiling

Open Shelves

Storage

10' 0" Flat Ceiling

Dining
14' 6" x 14' 6" Avg.
13' 4"h. Stepped Ceiling

Entry
13' 4" Flat Ceiling

Guest Suite 1
14' 4" x 14' 4"
10' 0"h. Flat Ceiling

WH

Drip Dry Rack

Studio
Iron Station
Duet W/D   SpaSink

A/C

A/C

3 Car Garage
22' 0" x 36' 6" Avg.
12' 0"h. Flat Ceiling

PLAN | *6750a The Cardiff*

3 Bedroom

3-1/2 Bath

Width: 101'4"

Depth: 106'0"

Exterior Walls: 8" CBS

Living Area: 3,883 sq ft

Foundation: Slab

Price Code: **PSE5**

Includes Whirlpool® Family Studio

PHOTO ABOVE: *Upon finishing a sumptuous meal, dinner guests can retire to the close-in living room, for a drink and views of the lanai.*

Please note: Home photographed may differ from blueprint.
Not available for construction in Lee or Collier Counties, Florida.

Photography: William C. Minarich

PHOTO ABOVE: *Equally at home nestled among pines or palms, this charming, rambling farmhouse design beautifully blends the traditional with the contemporary. Revival-style turrets flank the recessed entry porch, where graceful arches supported by decorative columns beckon to visitors across well-tended gardens.*

PHOTO RIGHT: *Interior lighting seems almost redundant in this spectacular foyer, where sunlight streams in through great expanses of glass to then be reflected downward by a sky-high ceiling.*

PHOTO FAR RIGHT: *Natural light plays a major role, not just in the foyer, but in the common zone created by the leisure room and kitchen, where the walls take on a golden hue.*

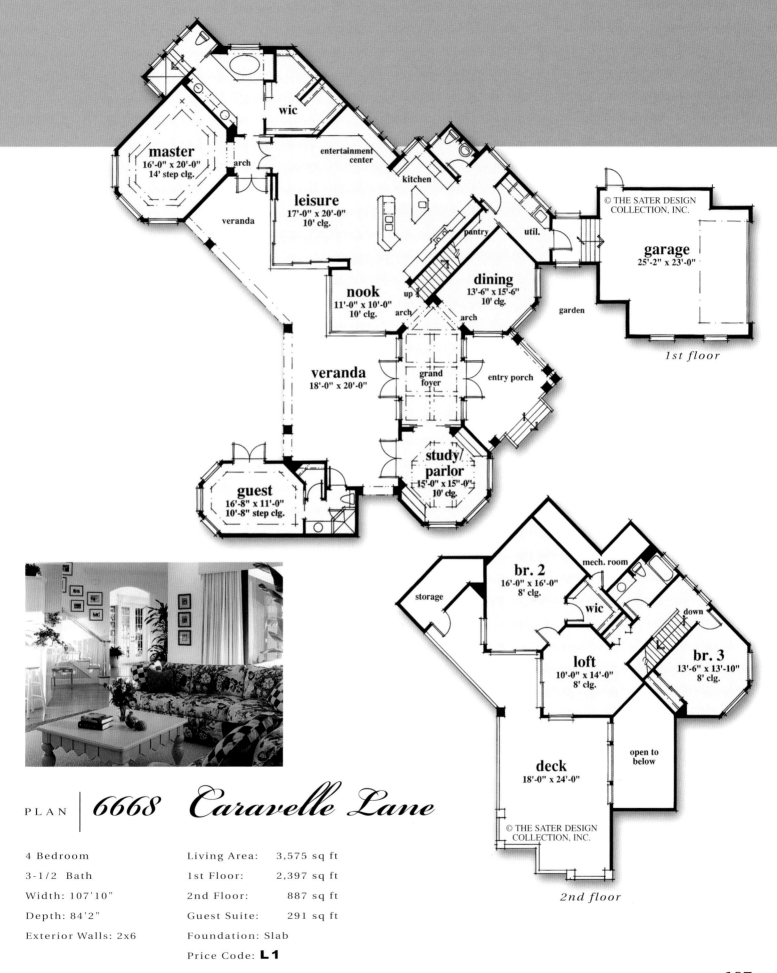

master
16'-0" x 20'-0"
14' step clg.

wic

entertainment center

kitchen

leisure
17'-0" x 20'-0"
10' clg.

arch

veranda

pantry

util.

© THE SATER DESIGN COLLECTION, INC.

garage
25'-2" x 23'-0"

nook
11'-0" x 10'-0"
10' clg.

up

dining
13'-6" x 15'-6"
10' clg.

arch

arch

garden

1st floor

veranda
18'-0" x 20'-0"

grand foyer

entry porch

guest
16'-8" x 11'-0"
10'-8" step clg.

study/ parlor
15'-0" x 15'-0"
10' clg.

storage

br. 2
16'-0" x 16'-0"
8' clg.

mech. room

wic

down

loft
10'-0" x 14'-0"
8' clg.

br. 3
13'-6" x 13'-10"
8' clg.

deck
18'-0" x 24'-0"

open to below

© THE SATER DESIGN COLLECTION, INC.

2nd floor

PLAN | *6668* *Caravelle Lane*

4 Bedroom	Living Area: 3,575 sq ft
3-1/2 Bath	1st Floor: 2,397 sq ft
Width: 107'10"	2nd Floor: 887 sq ft
Depth: 84'2"	Guest Suite: 291 sq ft
Exterior Walls: 2x6	Foundation: Slab
	Price Code: **L1**

Please note: Home photographed may differ from blueprint.

Photography: Oscar Thompson

PHOTO ABOVE: *Stunningly drenched in bright afternoon sun, this symmetrical modern Mediterranean combines the best of both worlds. One Old World element is a rich Mediterranean heritage, expressed in its columns, arches and turrets. The New World aspect is its view-oriented open floor plan, a design that caters to the needs and desires of the modern family.*

PHOTO ABOVE: *Seven-hundred-square-feet of covered lanai create a rambling, wraparound adult playground. When "snack time" comes, there's no need to panic — just head for the outdoor kitchen.*

PHOTO ABOVE: *Natural light streams into the living room through sliding glass doors. A charming corner fireplace (to the right) keeps guests cozy and warm on a cool evening.*

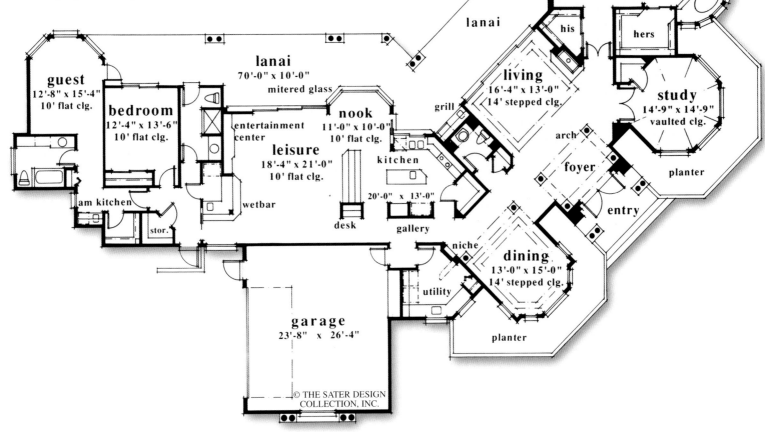

© THE SATER DESIGN COLLECTION, INC.

PLAN | *6640* *Castlepines Trace*

3 Bedroom

3-1/2 Bath

Width: 120'0"

Depth: 89'0"

Exterior Walls: 2x6

Living Area: 3,866 sq ft

Foundation: Slab

Price Code: **L1**

Please note: Home photographed may differ from blueprint.

Photography: Oscar Thompson

PHOTO ABOVE: *As regal as it is, the façade of this contemporary resort home sets the stage for an even more impressive performance within. Once inside, its charming, cottage-like appearance gives way to spacious rooms with volume ceilings, augmented by design features and details such as second-story balconies and turrets, vast expanses of panoramic views, decorative columns and elaborate balustrades.*

PHOTO RIGHT: *Inspired by the Roman loggia, this two-story series of arches supported by columns serves as a walkway to the second-story master suite, as well as a gallery that offers spectacular views of the grand living below.*

PHOTO FAR RIGHT: *Stunning two-story glass windows and a soaring twenty-two-foot, coffered ceiling bring this formal living room to new heights of luxury and spaciousness.*

PHOTO ABOVE: *This majestic rear elevation — spacious, stately and suggestive of a Tuscan vacation villa — could easily offer stunning late-afternoon views of hillside vineyards and ancient olive gardens.*

PHOTO RIGHT: *Fresh tomatoes, prosciutto, mozzarella, a loaf of ciabatta... just some of the food items that would find themselves right at home in this Romanesque gourmet kitchen.*

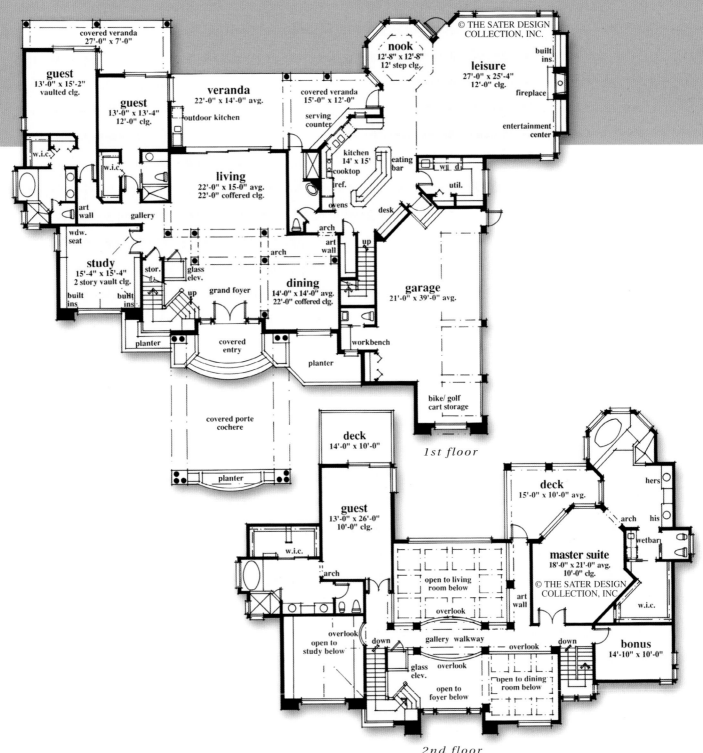

© THE SATER DESIGN COLLECTION, INC.

nook
12'-8" x 12'-8"
12' step clg.

leisure
27'-0" x 25'-4"
12'-0" clg.

built ins

fireplace

entertainment center

covered veranda
27'-0" x 7'-0"

guest
13'-0" x 15'-2"
vaulted clg.

guest
13'-0" x 13'-4"
12'-0" clg.

veranda
22'-0" x 14'-0" avg.

outdoor kitchen

covered veranda
15'-0" x 12'-0"

serving counter

w.i.c.

w.i.c.

living
22'-0" x 15'-0" avg.
22'-0" coffered clg.

kitchen
14' x 15'
cooktop

ref.

ovens

eating bar

wll dr

util.

art wall

gallery

wdw. seat

study
15'-4" x 15'-4"
2 story vault clg.

built ins

built ins

stor.

glass elev.

up

grand foyer

planter

up

arch

art wall

arch

dining
14'-0" x 14'-0" avg.
22'-0" coffered clg.

desk

garage
21'-0" x 39'-0" avg.

workbench

planter

bike/ golf cart storage

covered entry

covered porte cochere

planter

1st floor

deck
14'-0" x 10'-0"

guest
13'-0" x 26'-0"
10'-0" clg.

w.i.c.

arch

overlook
open to study below

open to living room below

overlook

down

glass elev.

open to foyer below

gallery walkway

overlook

deck
15'-0" x 10'-0" avg.

hers

arch

his

wetbar

master suite
18'-0" x 21'-0" avg.
10'-0" clg.

© THE SATER DESIGN COLLECTION, INC

art wall

w.i.c.

overlook

down

open to dining room below

bonus
14'-10" x 10'-0"

2nd floor

PLAN | **6732** *Old Cypress Pointe*

4 Bedroom	Living Area: 5,529 sq ft
5-1/2 Bath	1st Floor: 3,667 sq ft
Width: 102'0"	2nd Floor: 1,862 sq ft
Depth: 87'0"	Foundation: Slab
Exterior Walls: 8" CBS	Price Code: **PSE5**

Please note: Home photographed may differ from blueprint.

PLAN | *6633* *Royal Troon*

Photography: Laurence Taylor

PHOTO ABOVE: *Two pairs of slender decorative columns support a graceful arch, providing the defining characteristic of this contemporary Mediterranean — its grand recess entry.*

PHOTO RIGHT: *Nestled between the master suite and the foyer and bathed in light from three bay windows, this octagonal hideaway is a "study" in comfort and quietude.*

PHOTO ABOVE: *Zero-corner sliding glass doors at eye level, and stylish windows at sky level, all but eliminate the need for interior lighting in the formal living room.*

PHOTO LEFT: *This lanai pool is an integral part of the interior landscape and, with sliding glass doors open, as much a part of the floor plan as the adjacent breakfast nook.*

PHOTO ABOVE: *Outdoor entertaining never looked so inviting. The illuminated pool serves as a serene, and scenic, centerpiece for outdoor gatherings on the spacious lanai.*

PHOTO RIGHT: *Extremely family-friendly, the kitchen's ample island breakfast counter easily seats a student or two who has homework to do.*

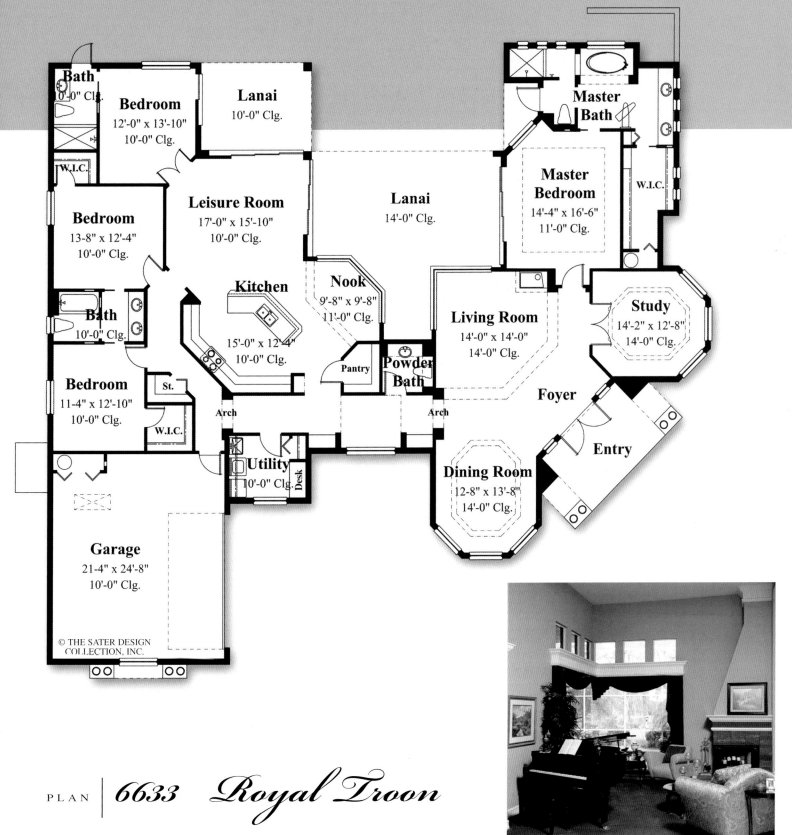

Bath
10'-0" Clg.

Bedroom
12'-0" x 13'-10"
10'-0" Clg.

Lanai
10'-0" Clg.

W.I.C.

Master Bath

Bedroom
13-8" x 12'-4"
10'-0" Clg.

Leisure Room
17'-0" x 15'-10"
10'-0" Clg.

Lanai
14'-0" Clg.

Master Bedroom
14'-4" x 16'-6"
11'-0" Clg.

W.I.C.

Bath
10'-0" Clg.

Kitchen
15'-0" x 12'-4"
10'-0" Clg.

Nook
9'-8" x 9'-8"
11'-0" Clg.

Living Room
14'-0" x 14'-0"
14'-0" Clg.

Study
14'-2" x 12'-8"
14'-0" Clg.

Bedroom
11'-4" x 12'-10"
10'-0" Clg.

St.

W.I.C.

Arch

Pantry

Powder Bath

Arch

Foyer

Entry

Utility
10'-0" Clg.

Desk

Dining Room
12-8" x 13'-8"
14'-0" Clg.

Garage
21-4" x 24'-8"
10'-0" Clg.

© THE SATER DESIGN
COLLECTION, INC.

PLAN | *6633* *Royal Troon*

4 Bedroom

3-1/2 Bath

Width: 82'8"

Depth: 76'4"

Exterior Walls: 8" CBS

Living Area: 2,986 sq ft

Foundation: Slab

Price Code: **C3**

PHOTO ABOVE: *The formal living room boasts sliding glass doors in one corner and a charming slate fireplace in the other.*

Please note: Home photographed may differ from blueprint.

PLAN | *6941* *Jasper Park*

Photography: Bruce Schaeffer

PHOTO ABOVE: *Three pairs of keystone pillars give this villa a symmetry and strength that, true to its Spanish roots, offer a proud sense of bravado. Powerful and angular, its countenance lets those who pass know that the privacy of those within is well protected.*

PHOTO RIGHT: *In contrast to the home's angular façade, the interior is softened by graceful arches and ornate columns, seen here in the entry to the formal dining room.*

PHOTO ABOVE: *Softer lines continue into the formal dining room, where decorative corbels set in a carved, arched coffer give this opulent setting an aura of intimacy.*

PHOTO ABOVE: *Peaceful arches in the gourmet kitchen have a soothing, calming effect — just what's needed most in the early morning hours.*

PHOTO ABOVE: *In the master bath, custom built-ins offer abundant storage space while high ceilings offer ample personal space.*

PHOTO ABOVE: *Surrounded by views of a lush garden and cascading waterfalls, this reclusive master bath is an absolute paradise on earth.*

PHOTO ABOVE: *The perfect place for roasting marshmallows, an octagonal gazebo is built into the covered lanai and features a stone fire pit.*

TOP PHOTO OPPOSITE PAGE: *Decorative columns support the sky-high ceiling of a generous covered lanai — complete with outdoor kitchen — that hugs the home's rear elevation.*

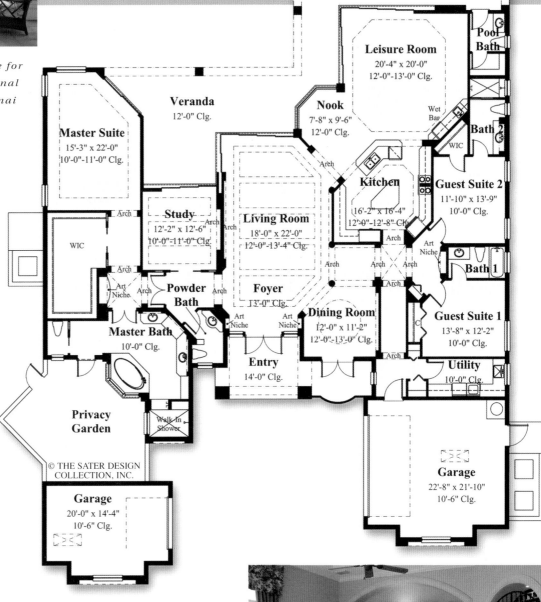

Firepit

Vaulted Clg.

Veranda
12'-0" Clg.

Outdoor Kitchen

Pool Bath

Leisure Room
20'-4" x 20'-0"
12'-0"-13'-0" Clg.

Wet Bar

Bath 2

Master Suite
15'-3" x 22'-0"
10'-0"-11'-0" Clg.

Veranda
12'-0" Clg.

Nook
7'-8" x 9'-6"
12'-0" Clg.

Arch

Guest Suite 2
11'-10" x 13'-9"
10'-0" Clg.

WIC

Study
12'-2" x 12'-6"
10'-0"-11'-0" Clg.

Kitchen
16'-2" x 16'-4"
12'-0"-12'-8" Clg.

Arch

Art Niche

Arch

Living Room
18'-0" x 22'-0"
12'-0"-13'-4" Clg.

Arch

Arch

Bath 1

WIC

Powder Bath

Art Niche

Arch

Foyer
13'-0" Clg.

Arch

Arch

Arch

Art Niche

Guest Suite 1
13'-8" x 12'-2"
10'-0" Clg.

Master Bath
10'-0" Clg.

Art Niche

Art Niche

Dining Room
12'-0" x 11'-2"
12'-0"-13'-0" Clg.

C

Arch

Entry
14'-0" Clg.

Utility
10'-0" Clg.

Walk In Shower

Privacy Garden

© THE SATER DESIGN COLLECTION, INC.

Garage
22'-8" x 21'-10"
10'-6" Clg.

Garage
20'-0" x 14'-4"
10'-6" Clg.

PLAN | **6941** *Jasper Park*

3 Bedroom

3 Full & 2 Half Baths

Width: 77'0"

Depth: 114'5"

Exterior Walls: 8" CBS

Living Area: 3,674 sq ft

Foundation: Slab

Price Code: **PSE5**

PHOTO ABOVE: *At the end of a hectic day, a comfortable chair — a short hop from the wet bar — can serve as a restful retreat in the leisure room.*

Please note: Home photographed may differ from blueprint. Not available for construction in Lee or Collier Counties, Florida.

Photography: CJ Walker

PHOTO ABOVE: *A stately cupola atop the entry portico keeps watch over the sprawling lawn and colorful gardens of the front elevation, while creating a lofty focal point for the façade of this Revival-style home.*

PHOTO RIGHT: *In architectural design circles, it may be a portico, but to some it's just a good old-fashioned front porch — a great place to relax in a favorite chair and watch the world go by.*

PHOTO ABOVE: *Formal, yet still friendly, this lovely living room offers a warm welcome to those who enter. A trio of floor-to-ceiling windows invite the outdoors in, treating guests to scenic panoramas of the exterior landscape.*

PHOTO LEFT: *After dark, the covered lanai glows and glitters, reflected lights dance on the surface of the tranquil turquoise pool.*

PHOTO ABOVE: *Leisure room, breakfast nook and gourmet kitchen flow into one another, creating an expansive family area that is both fashionable and functional... not to mention, fun.*

PHOTO RIGHT: *Double doors open from the master suite onto a breezy lanai. A master foyer connects the suite to spacious "His" and "Her" walk-in closets and then to a lavish master bath.*

PHOTO FAR RIGHT: *This study can be either a place to work, or a place to relax after work. In either scenario, it serves the purpose beautifully.*

PHOTO BOTTOM LEFT:

A gorgeous garden tub serves as the centerpiece of the master bath. On either side, are elegant "His" and "Her" vanities.

PHOTO BOTTOM RIGHT:

A starry sky appears through the bay windows of the formal dining room, serving guests a breathtaking view along with their dinner.

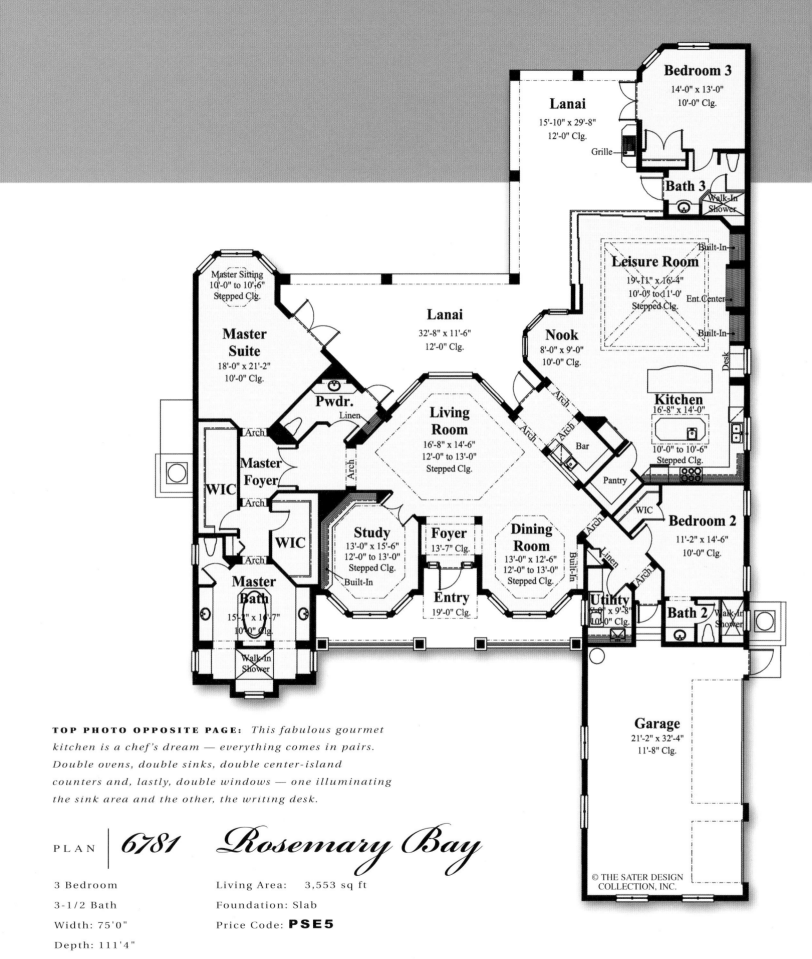

Bedroom 3
14'-0" x 13'-0"
10'-0" Clg.

Lanai
15'-10" x 29'-8"
12'-0" Clg.

Grille

Bath 3

Walk-In Shower

Leisure Room
19'-11" x 16'-4"
10'-0" to 11'-0"
Stepped Clg.

Built-In

Ent.Center

Built-In

Master Sitting
10'-0" to 10'-6"
Stepped Clg.

Lanai
32'-8" x 11'-6"
12'-0" Clg.

Nook
8'-0" x 9'-0"
10'-0" Clg.

Desk

Master Suite
18'-0" x 21'-2"
10'-0" Clg.

Pwdr.

Linen

Living Room
16'-8" x 14'-6"
12'-0" to 13'-0"
Stepped Clg.

Kitchen
16'-8" x 14'-0"
10'-0" to 10'-6"
Stepped Clg.

Arch

Arch

Bar

Master Foyer

Arch

Arch

Pantry

WIC

WIC

Arch

WIC

Arch

Study
13'-0" x 15'-6"
12'-0" to 13'-0"
Stepped Clg.
Built-In

Foyer
13'-7" Clg.

Dining Room
13'-0" x 12'-6"
12'-0" to 13'-0"
Stepped Clg.

Bedroom 2
11'-2" x 14'-6"
10'-0" Clg.

Linen

Arch

Arch

Built-In

Master Bath
15'-2" x 14'-7"
10'-0" Clg.

Entry
19'-0"

Utility
5'-0" x 9'-8"
10'-0" Clg.

Bath 2

Walk-In Shower

Walk-In Shower

Garage
21'-2" x 32'-4"
11'-8" Clg.

TOP PHOTO OPPOSITE PAGE: *This fabulous gourmet kitchen is a chef's dream — everything comes in pairs. Double ovens, double sinks, double center-island counters and, lastly, double windows — one illuminating the sink area and the other, the writing desk.*

© THE SATER DESIGN COLLECTION, INC.

PLAN | *6781* *Rosemary Bay*

3 Bedroom

3-1/2 Bath

Width: 75'0"

Depth: 111'4"

Exterior Walls: 8" CBS

Living Area: 3,553 sq ft

Foundation: Slab

Price Code: **PSE5**

*Please note: Home photographed may differ from blueprint.
Not for sale in Lee or Collier Counties, Florida.*

Photography: Oscar Thompson

PHOTO ABOVE: *A work of modern art, this rambling contemporary villa both complements and contrasts beautifully with its surroundings. The pinnacle of its towering, two-story roof pierces the sky, defining its unique façade and creating an interior space that is as grand and impressive as its exterior.*

PHOTO RIGHT: *A work of art in itself, the foyer sets the tone for an interior that is right out of a sleek, contemporary museum.*

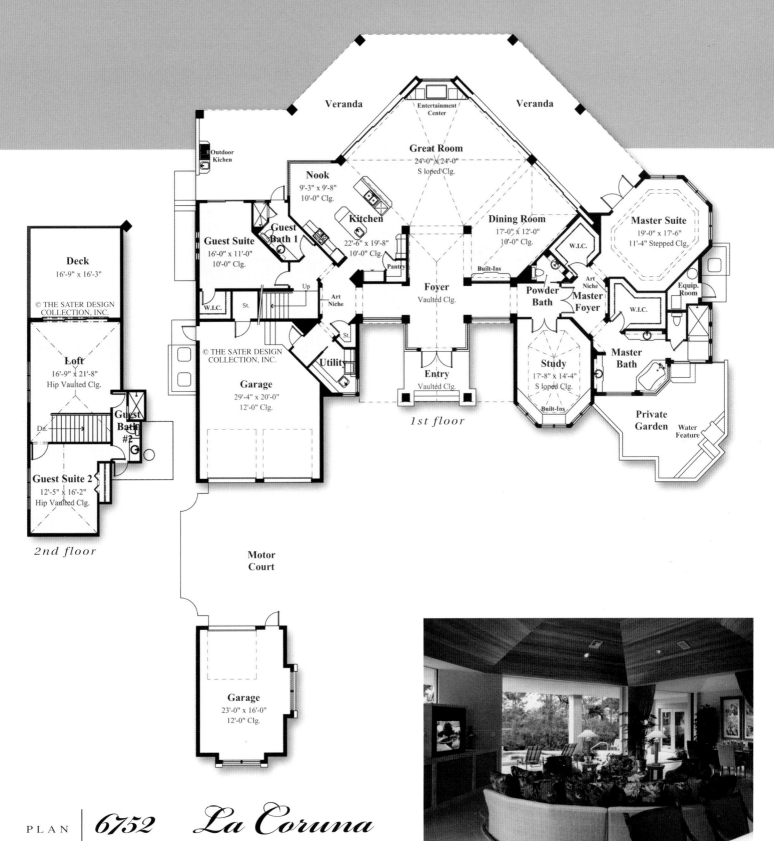

Deck
16'-9" x 16'-3"

© THE SATER DESIGN
COLLECTION, INC.

Loft
16'-9" x 21'-8"
Hip Vaulted Clg.

Dn.

Guest
Bath
#2

Guest Suite 2
12'-5" x 16'-2"
Hip Vaulted Clg.

2nd floor

Veranda

Entertainment
Center

Veranda

Outdoor
Kichen

Great Room
24'-0" x 24'-0"
Sloped Clg.

Nook
9'-3" x 9'-8"
10'-0" Clg.

Kitchen
22'-6" x 19'-8"
10'-0" Clg.

Dining Room
17'-0" x 12'-0"
10'-0" Clg.

Master Suite
19'-0" x 17'-6"
11'-4" Stepped Clg.

Guest Suite
16'-0" x 11'-0"
10'-0" Clg.

Guest
Bath 1

W.I.C.

Pantry

Built-Ins

W.I.C.

Art
Niche

Equip.
Room

W.I.C.

St.

Up

Art
Niche

Foyer
Vaulted Clg.

Powder
Bath

Master
Foyer

W.I.C.

Master
Bath

© THE SATER DESIGN
COLLECTION, INC.

Utility

St.

Garage
29'-4" x 20'-0"
12'-0" Clg.

Entry
Vaulted Clg.

Study
17'-8" x 14'-4"
Sloped Clg.

Built-Ins

Private
Garden

Water
Feature

1st floor

Motor
Court

Garage
23'-0" x 16'-0"
12'-0" Clg.

PLAN | *6752* *La Coruna*

3 Bedroom

3-1/2 Bath

Width: 99'10"

Depth: 139'11"

Exterior Walls: 8" CBS

Living Area: 4,398 sq ft

1st Floor: 3,741 sq ft

2nd Floor: 657 sq ft

Foundation: Slab

Price Code: **PSE5**

PHOTO ABOVE: *The epitome of spaciousness, the great room blends a soaring ceiling and spectacular views with a space that defines family-friendly.*

Please note: Home photographed may differ from blueprint.

Discover the Essential Ingredient.

They say the kitchen is the soul of the home. And so it should be — a place where you show off your culinary talents and exceptional good taste. KitchenAid® appliances meet the desires of the passionate cook with appliances that suit any design. Whether your new kitchen recreates the look of a French bistro or a rustic farmhouse, KitchenAid® appliances can provide both the performance and styling you're looking for.

KitchenAid® offers a wide range of appliances for the entire kitchen — from wine cellars to commercial-style ranges to drawer dishwashers. You can also select KitchenAid® sinks and faucets that offer the same high level of quality, as well as unique products such as the KitchenAid® briva® in-sink dishwasher that functions as both a sink and small dishwasher.

PHOTO AT TOP: *KitchenAid® Pro Line™ Series appliances, with their matte meteorite finish and distinctive handles and instrumentation, add sophistication to this kitchen design.*

PHOTO ABOVE: *The versatile briva® in-sink dishwasher is an ideal companion to a full-size dishwasher. Place a cutting board on top and it's also a food-staging area.*

For complete product information and specifications:
www.kitchenaid.com   1.800.422.1230

PHOTO ABOVE: *Integrate appliances with your kitchen design using KitchenAid® appliances. The KitchenAid® Architect® Series refrigerator and drawer dishwasher shown here feature custom door panels and are complemented with a commercial-style range and powerful hood liner.*

For complete product information and specifications:
www.kitchenaid.com   1.800.422.1230

PHOTO AT TOP: *Your meals will never taste better than when they are prepared on a KitchenAid® outdoor grill. This model features a separate gas burner, convenient for preparing sauces and side dishes.*

PHOTO ABOVE: *The KitchenAid® outdoor refreshment center provides a convenient serving station as part of a complete KitchenAid® outdoor kitchen.*

MAIN PHOTO: *Here's another perfect setting for a KitchenAid® outdoor kitchen. The commercial-style outdoor grill is complemented by the built-in refreshment center and refrigerator, situated close to an area for outdoor dining.*

For complete product information and specifications:
www.kitchenaid.com   1.800.422.1230

Outdoor entertaining is becoming an essential element of home design. So in planning your outdoor kitchen, it makes sense to consider the same lifestyle and cooking performance considerations as you would for your indoor kitchen.

KitchenAid® brand appliances demonstrate the same legendary performance with a comprehensive line of outdoor appliances. Select from built-in or freestanding grills, refrigerators, ice makers and serving carts — all constructed in durable stainless steel. Combine these commercial-style outdoor appliances with your choice of brick, stone, stucco, wood or concrete block, and you have an attractive outdoor kitchen that stands up to the elements and allows you to entertain outdoors.

KitchenAid®
HOME APPLIANCES

The Best Garage on the Block.™

A workbench provides a handy work surface for home improvement and craft projects—with space to dock up to three Gladiator™ modules underneath.

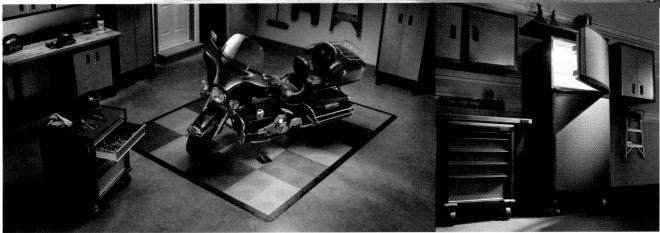

Now your garage can be as impressive as the rest of your home with Gladiator™ GarageWorks by Whirlpool Corporation. This unique product line includes sturdy wall-storage options, workbenches, tool and gear cabinets, and innovative floor covering for a complete finished look. The sleek tread - plate design found on Gladiator™ products creates a pleasing aesthetic unmatched by other garage organization products. With Gladiator™ GarageWorks, your garage works for you and creates a space that will be the envy of your friends and neighbors.

MAIN PHOTO: *Choose from the complete system to design the garage of your dreams. Included are the Freezerator® convertible refrigerator/freezer, Modular Workbench, Tall GearBox and Tall GearBox Lockers, Modular GearBox and GearDrawer Cabinets. GearWall® Panels mean you can hang cabinets anywhere as well as use shelving, hooks and accessories for arranging tools and more.*

PHOTO AT LEFT: *Attractive raise-tile floor covering can add protection and styling to your garage, as part of the Gladiator™ GarageWorks system.*

PHOTO ABOVE: *Gladiator™ GarageWorks features the Freezerator™ (center), a dual-function refrigerator/freezer suitable for the garage environment, as well as heavy-duty flooring that complements the look of the cabinets and storage units.*

For complete product information and specifications:
www.gladiatorgw.com 1.800.253.1301

PHOTO ABOVE: *This Family Studio incorporates innovative Whirlpool® fabric-care products with a computer workstation — for an attractive multi-functional space. The Duet® Fabric Care System is shown with optional pedestals.*

When is a laundry room not just a laundry room? When it's a Whirlpool® Family Studio. This exciting new concept in home planning combines innovative, high-performance fabric-care products from Whirlpool Corporation and a multi-functional space. It's a place designed to make every day more productive as you clean and care for all your fabrics.

As an in-home fabric-care center, the Family Studio can incorporate whatever uses you desire, and can be situated where it makes sense within your home design — as an extension of your kitchen, on a lower level or upstairs near the bedrooms. Cabinets can conceal the fabric-care products when not in use for a clean, functional appearance.

For complete product information and specifications:
www.family-studio.com   1.800.253.1301

Redefining the Laundry Room.

PHOTO ABOVE: *This Whirlpool® Family Studio features (left to right) the ImPress™ Ironing Station, the SinkSpa™ Jetted Sink, the DryAire™ Drying Cabinet and the Duet® Washer and Dryer Pair.*

The Duet® Washer and Dryer pair are the cornerstone of any Whirlpool® Family Studio you choose to build in your new home. This pair of laundry appliances makes optimal use of your time caring for fabrics with its ENERGY STAR® qualified performance.

For complete product information and specifications:
www.family-studio.com   1.800.253.1301

East Lake Way

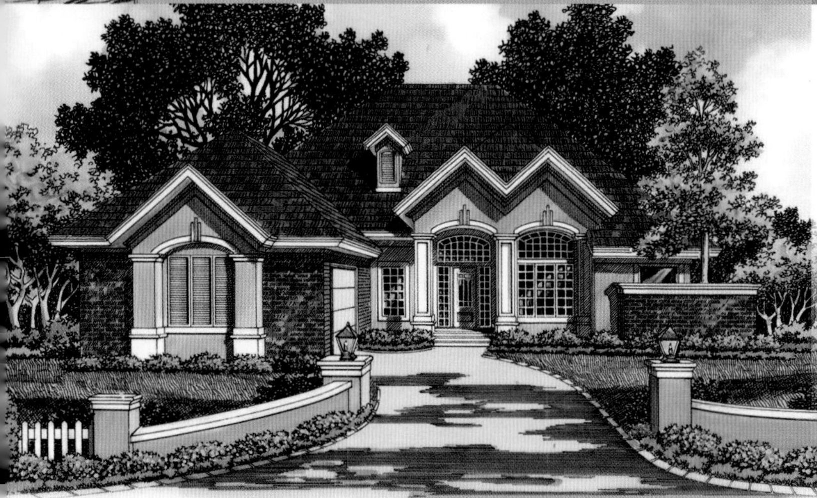

Plan 6711/*6714

3 Bed / 2-1/2 Bath
Living Area: 2,856 sq ft
Width: 63'4" / Depth: 87'0"
Exterior Walls: 2x6
Foundation: Slab
Price Code: **C3**

REAR ELEVATION

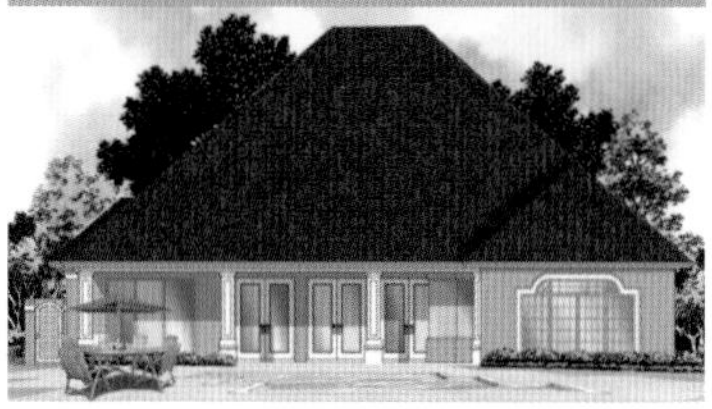

© THE SATER DESIGN COLLECTION, INC.

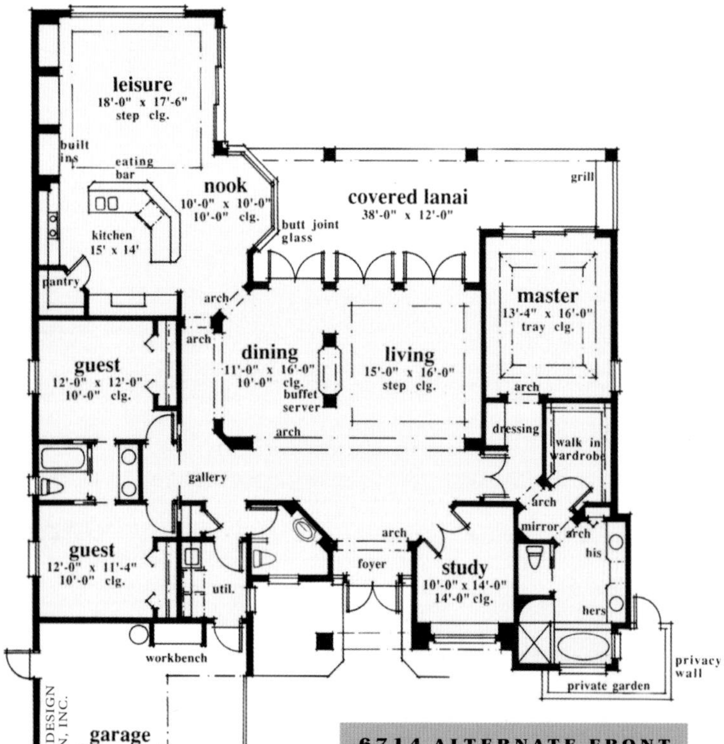

leisure
18'-0" x 17'-6"
step clg.
built ins
eating bar
nook
10'-0" x 10'-0"
10'-0" clg.
covered lanai
38'-0" x 12'-0"
grill
kitchen
15' x 14'
butt joint glass
pantry
arch
master
13'-4" x 16'-0"
tray clg.
guest
12'-0" x 12'-0"
10'-0" clg.
dining
11'-0" x 16'-0"
10'-0" clg.
buffet server
living
15'-0" x 16'-0"
step clg.
dressing
walk in wardrobe
gallery
mirror
his
guest
12'-0" x 11'-4"
10'-0" clg.
foyer
study
10'-0" x 14'-0"
14'-0" clg.
util.
hers
workbench
privacy wall
private garden
garage
22'-0" x 23'-4"
© THE SATER DESIGN COLLECTION, INC.

6714 ALTERNATE FRONT

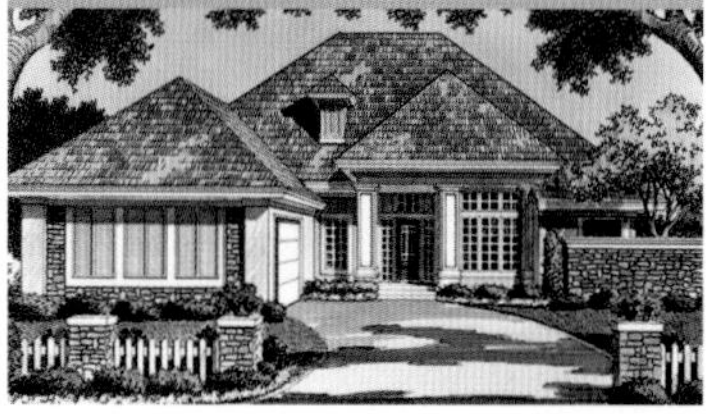

VISIT OUR WEBSITE FOR MORE INFORMATION

Annapolis Trail

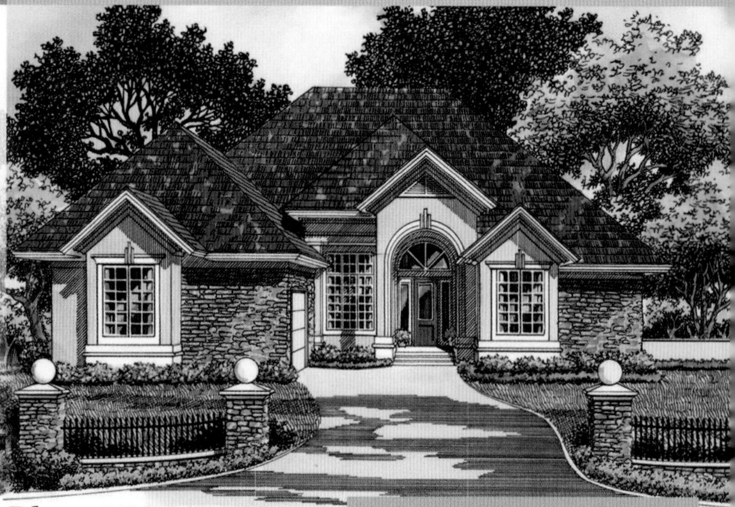

Plan 6720/*6726

3 Bed / 3 Bath
Living Area: 2,723 sq ft
Width: 62'0" / Depth: 80'4"
Exterior Walls: 8" CBS / 2x6
Foundation: Slab
Price Code: **C3**

REAR ELEVATION

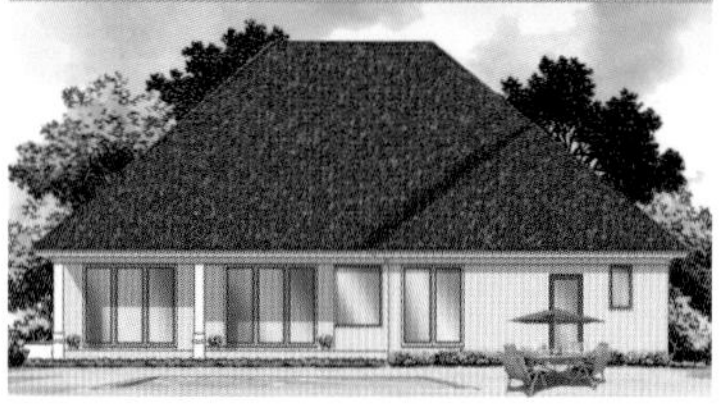

© THE SATER DESIGN COLLECTION, INC.

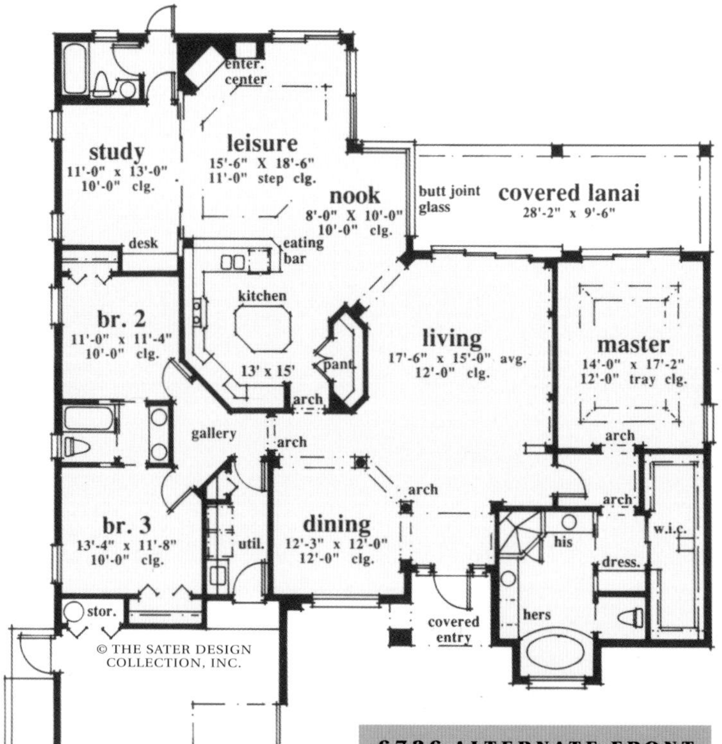

enter. center
study
11'-0" x 13'-0"
10'-0" clg.
leisure
15'-6" X 18'-6"
11'-0" step clg.
nook
8'-0" X 10'-0"
10'-0" clg.
butt joint glass
covered lanai
28'-2" x 9'-6"
desk
eating bar
kitchen
13' x 15'
pant.
br. 2
11'-0" x 11'-4"
10'-0" clg.
living
17'-6" x 15'-0" avg.
12'-0" clg.
master
14'-0" x 17'-2"
12'-0" tray clg.
arch
gallery
br. 3
13'-4" x 11'-8"
10'-0" clg.
util.
dining
12'-3" x 12'-0"
12'-0" clg.
his
w.i.c.
dress.
hers
stor.
covered entry
© THE SATER DESIGN COLLECTION, INC.
garage
20'-8" x 25'-0"

6726 ALTERNATE FRONT

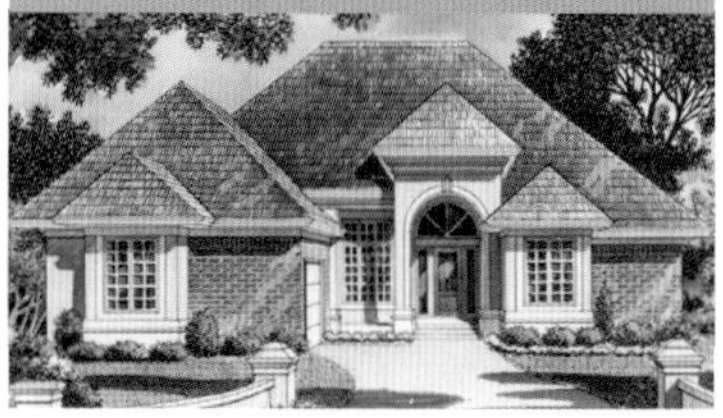

VISIT OUR WEBSITE FOR MORE INFORMATION

Royal Palm

Coral Harbor

Plan 6727

3 Bed / 2-1/2 Bath

Living Area: 2,823 sq ft

Width: 65'0" / Depth: 85'4"

Exterior Walls: 8" CBS

Foundation: Slab

Price Code: **C3**

REAR ELEVATION

© THE SATER DESIGN COLLECTION, INC.

Plan 6728

3 Bedroom / 3-1/2 Bath

Living Area: 3,696 sq ft

1st Floor: 3,258 sq ft

Guest Suite: 438 sq ft

Width: 80'0" / Depth: 107'3"

Exterior Walls: 8" CBS

Foundation: Slab

Price Code: **L1**

REAR ELEVATION

© THE SATER DESIGN COLLECTION, INC.

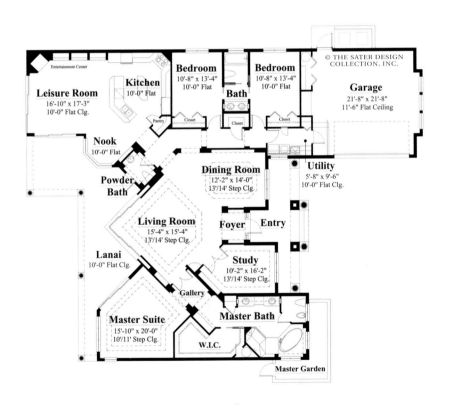

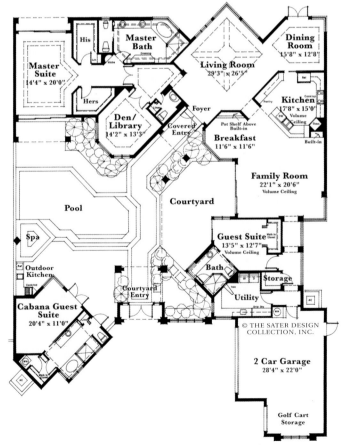

Griffith Parkway

Fiddler's Creek

Plan 6721/*6722

4 Bed / 3-1/2 Bath

Living Area: 3,872 sq ft

Width: 65'0" / Depth: 91'0"

Exterior Walls: 2x6

Foundation: Slab

Price Code: **L1**

REAR ELEVATION

© THE Sater DESIGN COLLECTION, INC.

1st Floor: 2,924 sq ft

2nd Floor: 948 sq ft

Plan 6746a

4 Bed / 3-1/2 Bath

Living Area: 3,893 sq ft

Width: 85'0" / Depth: 76'2"

Exterior Walls: 2x6

Foundation:
Slab or Opt. Basement

Price Code: **L1**

REAR ELEVATION

© THE Sater DESIGN COLLECTION, INC.

1st Floor: 2,841 sq ft

2nd Floor: 1,052 sq ft

Includes Whirlpool® Family Studio

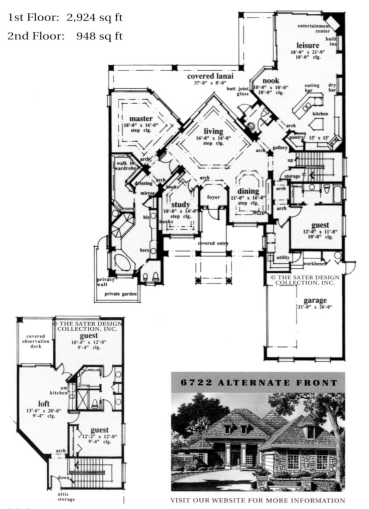

6722 ALTERNATE FRONT

VISIT OUR WEBSITE FOR MORE INFORMATION

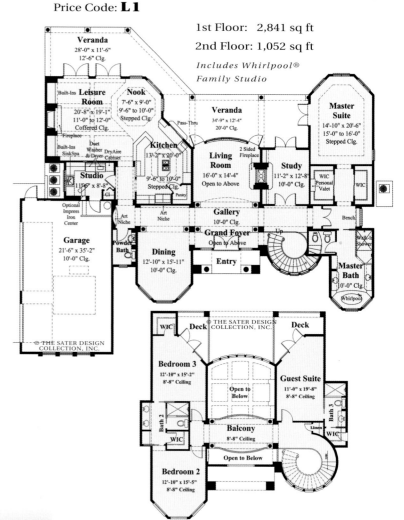

Queenstown Harbor

Plan 6663a

3 Bed / 3-1/2 Bath

Living Area: 2,978 sq ft

Width: 84'0" / Depth: 90'0"

Exterior Walls: 8" CBS or 2x6

Foundation: Slab

Price Code: **C3**

Includes Whirlpool™
Family Studio

REAR ELEVATION

© THE SATER DESIGN COLLECTION, INC.

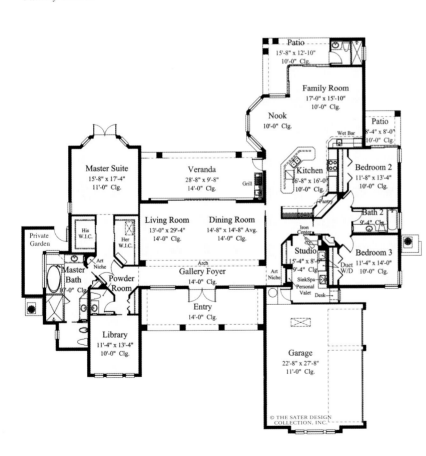

Hillcrest Ridge

Plan 6651a

4 Bed / 3-1/2 Bath

Living Area: 4,759 sq ft

Width: 95'4" / Depth: 83'0"

Exterior Walls: 2x6

Foundation: Basement

Price Code: **L3**

1st Floor: 3,546 sq ft

2nd Floor: 1,213 sq ft

Includes Whirlpool™
Family Studio

REAR ELEVATION

© THE SATER DESIGN COLLECTION, INC.

Plantation Pine

Whispering Pines

Plan 6735a

4 Bed / 5 Bath

Living Area: 4,296 sq ft

Guest Suite: 331 sq ft

Width: 88'0" / Depth: 119'0"

Depth w/guest suite: 133'0"

Exterior Walls: 8" CBS

Foundation: Slab

Price Code: **L2**

Includes Whirlpool™
Family Studio

REAR ELEVATION

© THE SATER DESIGN COLLECTION, INC.

Plan 6736

3 Bed / 3 Bath

Living Area: 3,599 sq ft

Width: 89'8" / Depth: 53'9"

Exterior Walls: 2x6

Foundation: Slab

Price Code: **L1**

1st Floor: 2,369 sq ft

2nd Floor: 1,230 sq ft

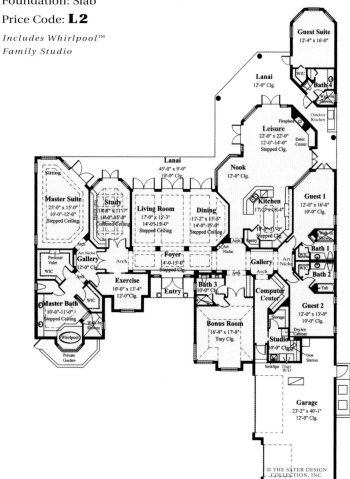

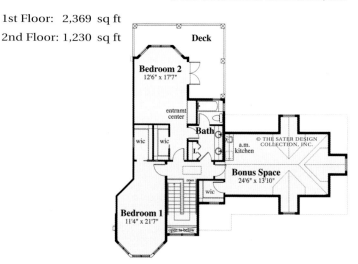

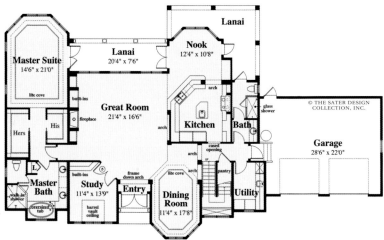

© THE SATER DESIGN COLLECTION, INC.

Lochwood Drive

Bay Landing Drive

Plan 6675

5 Bed / 3 Bath

Living Area: 3,285 sq ft

Width: 66'0" / Depth: 80'6"

Exterior Walls: 8" CBS

Foundation: Slab

Price Code: **C4**

REAR ELEVATION

© THE SATER DESIGN COLLECTION, INC.

1st Floor: 2,747 sq ft

2nd Floor: 538 sq ft

Plan 6676

3 Bed / 3-1/2 Bath

Living Area: 3,714 sq ft

Width: 85'4" / Depth: 91'0"

Exterior Walls: 8" CBS

Foundation: Slab

Price Code: **L1**

REAR ELEVATION

© THE SATER DESIGN COLLECTION, INC.

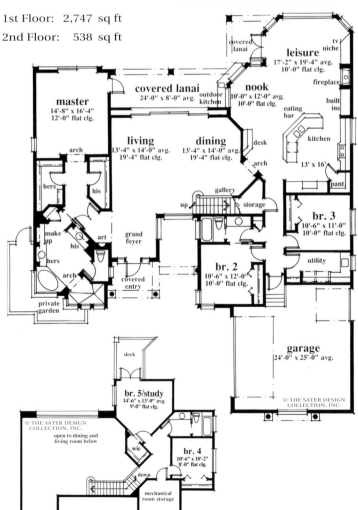

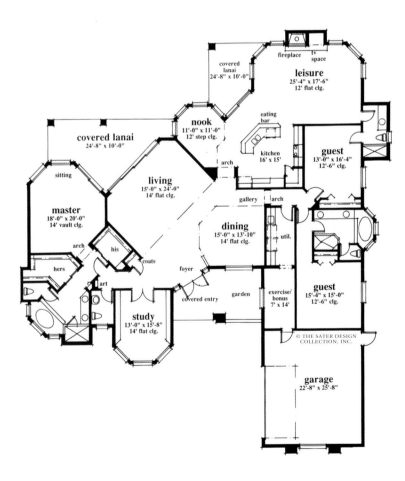

Waterford Place

Lucaya Cove

Plan 6647

4 Bed / 3 Full, 2 Half Bath

Living Area: 3,670 sq ft

Width: 80'4" / Depth: 65'4"

Exterior Walls: 8" CBS

Foundation: Slab

Price Code: **L1**

REAR ELEVATION

© THE SATER DESIGN COLLECTION, INC.

Plan 6648

4 Bed / 5 Bath

Living Area: 4,563 sq ft

Width: 54'8" / Depth: 97'4"

Exterior Walls: 8" CBS

Foundation: Slab

Price Code: **L2**

REAR ELEVATION

© THE SATER DESIGN COLLECTION, INC.

1st Floor: 2,638 sq ft

2nd Floor: 1,032 sq ft

1st Floor: 2,618 sq ft

2nd Floor: 1,945 sq ft

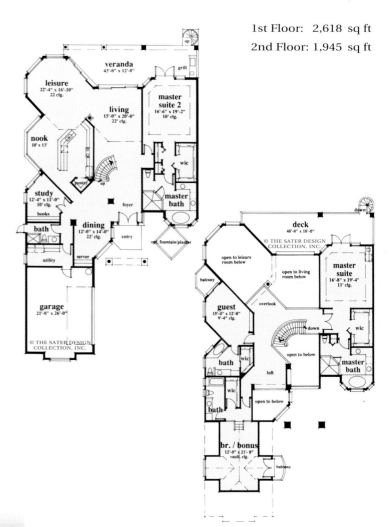

Cotton Creek Trace

Plan 6650

4 Bed / 4 Bath

Living Area: 3,748 sq ft

Width: 77'4" / Depth: 93'10"

Exterior Walls: 8" CBS

Foundation: Slab

Price Code: **L1**

REAR ELEVATION

© THE SATER DESIGN COLLECTION, INC.

1st Floor: 3,092 sq ft

2nd Floor: 656 sq ft

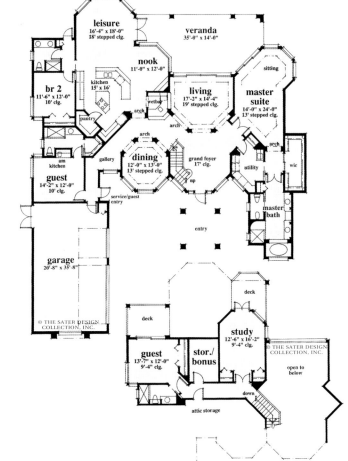

Stoney Creek Way

Plan 6656a

4 Bed / 3-1/2 Bath

Living Area: 4,140 sq ft

Width: 87'4" / Depth: 80'4"

Exterior Walls: 2x6

Foundation: Slab

Price Code: **L3**

REAR ELEVATION

© THE SATER DESIGN COLLECTION, INC.

1st Floor: 3,053 sq ft

2nd Floor: 1,087 sq ft

*Includes Whirlpool™
Family Studio*

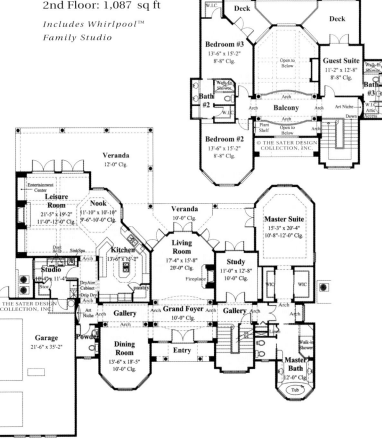

Royal Birkdale

Hermitage Place

Plan 6665

3 Bed / 3-1/2 Bath

Living Area: 3,279 sq ft

Width: 75'0" / Depth: 105'0"

Exterior Walls: 8" CBS

Foundation: Slab

Price Code: **C4**

REAR ELEVATION

© THE Sater DESIGN COLLECTION, INC.

Plan 6666

3 Bed / 3-1/2 Bath

Living Area: 3,229 sq ft

Width: 76'0" / Depth: 105'4"

Exterior Walls: 8" CBS

Foundation: Slab

Price Code: **C4**

REAR ELEVATION

© THE Sater DESIGN COLLECTION, INC.

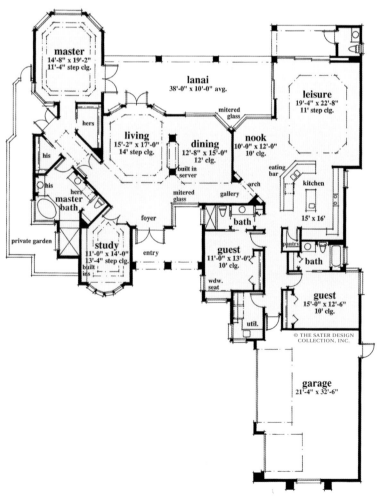

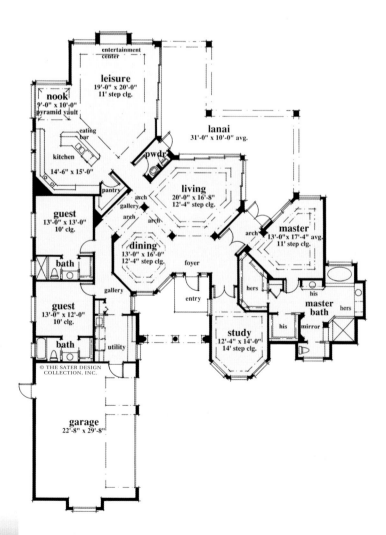

Oakmont Trace

Greenbriar Way

Plan 6611

3 Bed / 3 Full, 2 Half Bath

Living Area: 3,104 sq ft

Width: 73'0" / Depth: 108'0"

Exterior Walls: 8" CBS

Foundation: Slab

Price Code: **C4**

REAR ELEVATION

© THE SATER DESIGN COLLECTION, INC.

Plan 6609

3 Bed / 3 Bath

Living Area: 3,324 sq ft

Width: 74'0" / Depth: 89'8"

Exterior Walls: 8" CBS

Foundation: Slab

Price Code: **C4**

REAR ELEVATION

© THE SATER DESIGN COLLECTION, INC.

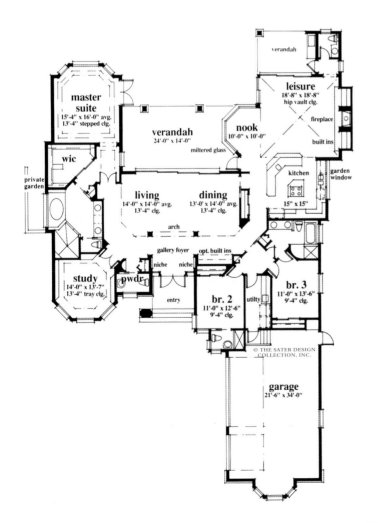

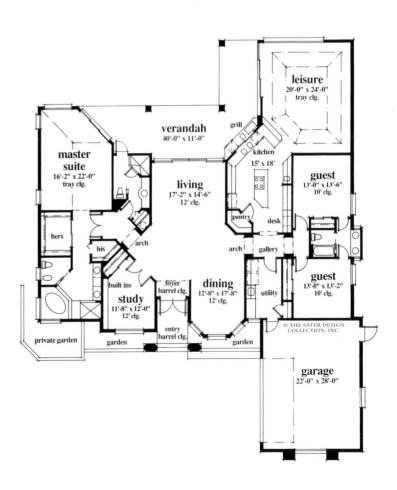

Anna Belle

Royal Country Down

Plan 6782

4 Bed / 4 Bath

Living Area: 4,091 sq ft

Width: 98'0" / Depth: 60'0"

Exterior Walls: 2x6

Foundation:
Slab or Crawlspace

Price Code: **L2**

1st Floor: 2,701 sq ft

2nd Floor: 1,390 sq ft

REAR ELEVATION

© THE Sater DESIGN COLLECTION, INC.

Plan 8001a

4 Bed / 3-1/2 Bath

Living Area: 3,977 sq ft

Width: 85'0" / Depth: 76'8"

Exterior Walls: 2x6

Foundation:
Slab or Optional Basement

Price Code: **L1**

1st Floor: 2,834 sq ft

2nd Floor: 1,143 sq ft

Includes Whirlpool® Family Studio

REAR ELEVATION

© THE Sater DESIGN COLLECTION, INC.

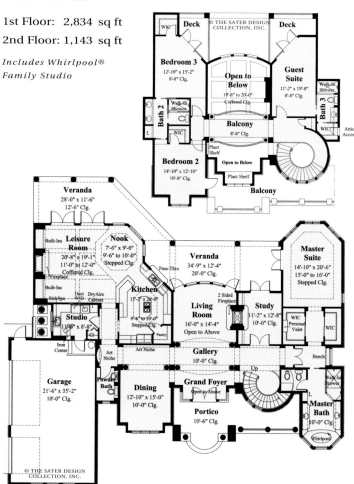

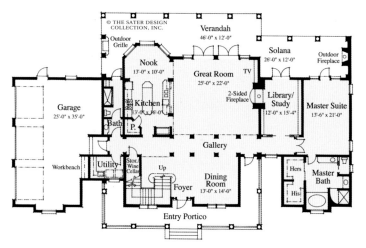

La Riviere

San Lorenzo

Plan 8011

4 Bed / 4-1/2 Bath

Living Area: 3,988 sq ft

Width: 71'6" / Depth: 83'0"

Exterior Walls: 2x6

Foundation:
Slab or Optional Basement

Price Code: **L2**

1st Floor: 2,830 sq ft

2nd Floor: 1,158 sq ft

Bonus: 371 sq ft

REAR ELEVATION

© THE SATER DESIGN COLLECTION, INC.

Plan 8014a/*8013

4 Bed / 4-1/2 Bath

Living Area: 4,664 sq ft

Width: 70'0" / Depth: 100'0"

Exterior Walls: 2x6

Foundation:
Slab or Optional Basement

Price Code: **L2**

1st Floor: 3,025 sq ft

2nd Floor: 1,639 sq ft

Bonus: 294 sq ft

*Includes Whirlpool®
Family Studio*

REAR ELEVATION

© THE SATER DESIGN COLLECTION, INC.

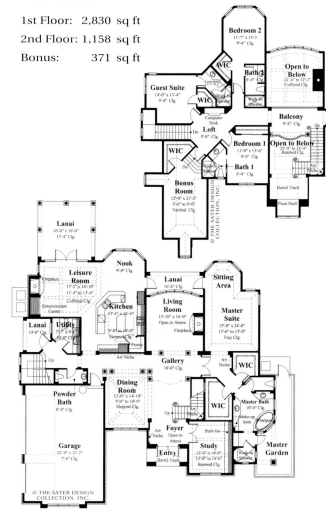

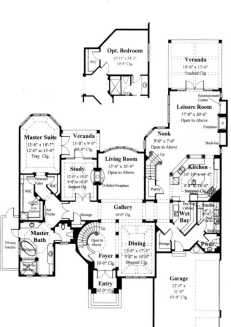

8013 ALTERNATE FRONT

VISIT OUR WEBSITE FOR MORE INFORMATION

Preston Trail

Brendan Cove

Plan 6739

3 Bed / 3 Full 2 Half Baths

Living Area: 5,407 sq ft

Width: 90'0" / Depth: 85'0"

Exterior Walls: 8" CBS

Foundation: Slab

Price Code: **L4**

1st Floor: 4,138 sq ft

2nd Floor: 1,269 sq ft

REAR ELEVATION

© THE SATER DESIGN COLLECTION, INC.

Plan 6740

4 Bed / 5 Bath

Living Area: 4,633 sq ft

Width: 76'8" / Depth: 113'0"

Exterior Walls: 8" CBS

Foundation: Slab

Price Code: **L2**

1st Floor: 3,670 sq ft

2nd Floor: 963 sq ft

REAR ELEVATION

© THE SATER DESIGN COLLECTION, INC.

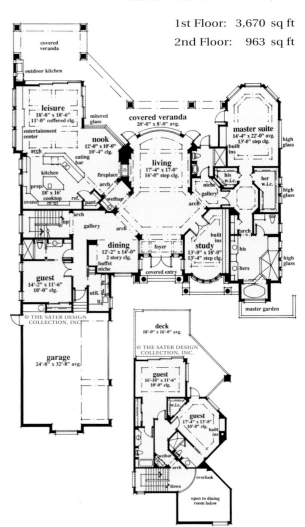

Stoney Creek Lane

Edgewood Court

Plan 6649

3 Bed / 3-1/2 Bath

Living Area: 3,980 sq ft

Width: 82'4" / Depth: 103'4"

Exterior Walls: 8" CBS

Foundation: **Slab**

Price Code: **L1**

REAR ELEVATION

© THE SATER DESIGN COLLECTION, INC.

1st Floor: 3,035 sq ft

2nd Floor: 945 sq ft

Plan 6646

3 Bed / 2-1/2 Bath

Living Area: 3,588 sq ft

Width: 76'0" / Depth: 90'0"

Exterior Walls: 8" CBS

Foundation: **Slab**

Price Code: **L1**

REAR ELEVATION

© THE SATER DESIGN COLLECTION, INC.

1st Floor: 2,551 sq ft

2nd Floor: 1,037 sq ft

Port Royal Way

Spring Hill Lane

Plan 6635a

5 Bed / 6-1/2 Bath

Living Area: 6,312 sq ft

Width: 98'0" / Depth: 103'8"

Exterior Walls: 8" CBS

Foundation: Slab

Price Code: **L4**

1st Floor: 4,760 sq ft

2nd Floor: 1,552 sq ft

Includes Whirlpool® Family Studio

REAR ELEVATION

© THE SATER DESIGN COLLECTION, INC.

Plan 6661

4 Bed / 3-1/2 Bath

Living Area: 3,301 sq ft

Width: 80'0" / Depth: 103'8"

Exterior Walls: 2x6 or 8" CBS

Foundation: Slab

Price Code: **C4**

REAR ELEVATION

© THE SATER DESIGN COLLECTION, INC.

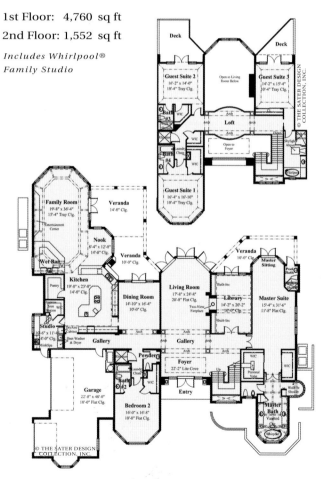

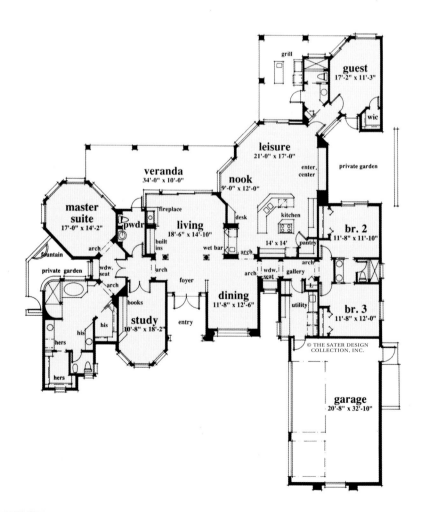

Plan 6679

3 Bed / 3 Bath

Living Area: 3,296 sq ft

Bonus Room: 407 sq ft

Width: 88'0" / Depth: 78'0"

Exterior Walls: 8" CBS

Foundation: Slab

Price Code: **C4**

REAR ELEVATION

© THE SATER DESIGN COLLECTION, INC.

Plan 6723/*6724

3 Bed / 3 Bath

Living Area: 2,891 sq ft

Width: 65'0" / Depth: 79'0"

Exterior Walls: 2x6

Foundation: Slab

Price Code: **C3**

REAR ELEVATION

© THE SATER DESIGN COLLECTION, INC.

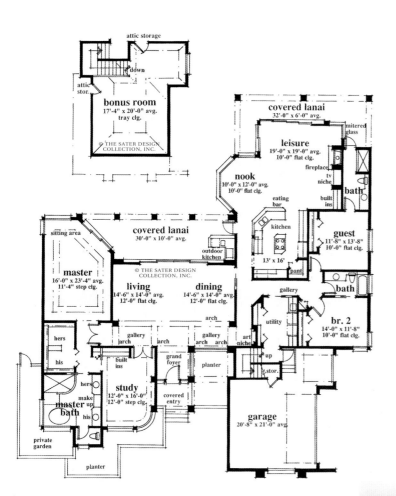

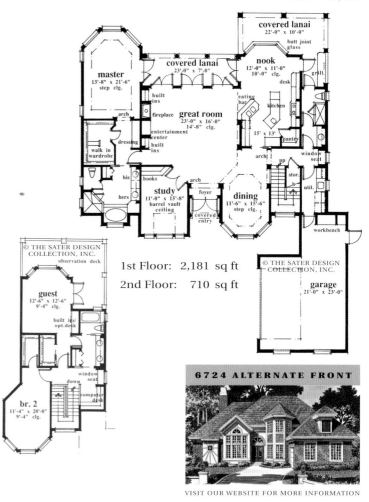

1st Floor: 2,181 sq ft

2nd Floor: 710 sq ft

6724 ALTERNATE FRONT

VISIT OUR WEBSITE FOR MORE INFORMATION

Aubrey

Bellamy

Plan 8016

4 Bed / 3-1/2 Bath

Living Area: 3,611 sq ft

Width: 83'0" / Depth: 71'8"

Exterior Walls: 2x6

Foundation:
Slab or Optional Basement

Price Code: **L1**

1st Floor: 2,484 sq ft

2nd Floor: 1,127 sq ft

Bonus: 332 sq ft

REAR ELEVATION

© THE SATER DESIGN COLLECTION, INC.

Plan 8018

4 Bed / 3-1/2 Bath

Living Area: 3,610 sq ft

Width: 83'0" / Depth: 71'8"

Exterior Walls: 2x6

Foundation:
Slab or Optional Basement

Price Code: **L1**

1st Floor: 2,483 sq ft

2nd Floor: 1,127 sq ft

Bonus: 332 sq ft

REAR ELEVATION

© THE SATER DESIGN COLLECTION, INC.

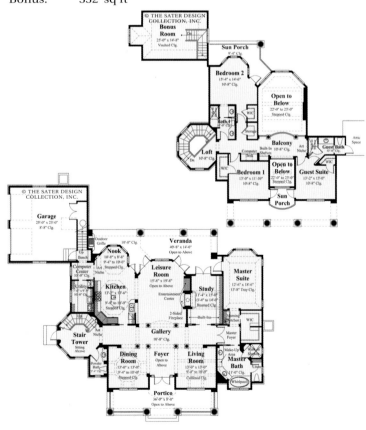

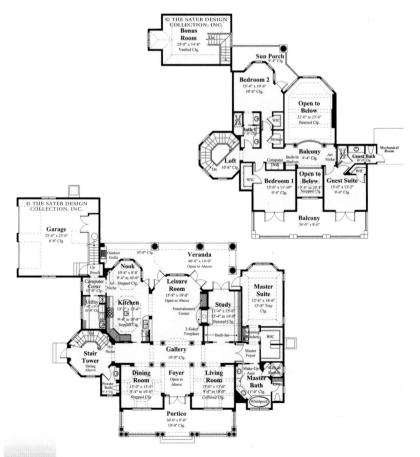

Brittany

Beauchamp

Plan 8040/*8041

3 Bed / 2 Full, 2 Half Bath

Living Area: 3,353 sq ft

Width: 84'0" / Depth: 92'0"

Exterior Walls: 2x6

Foundation: Slab

Price Code: **C4**

REAR ELEVATION

© THE SATER DESIGN COLLECTION, INC.

Plan 8044a/*8045

4 Bed / 3-1/2 Bath

Living Area: 3,790 sq ft

Width: 80'8" / Depth: 104'8"

Exterior Walls: 2x6

Foundation:
Slab or Optional Basement

Price Code: **L1**

Includes Whirlpool®
Family Studio

REAR ELEVATION

© THE SATER DESIGN COLLECTION, INC.

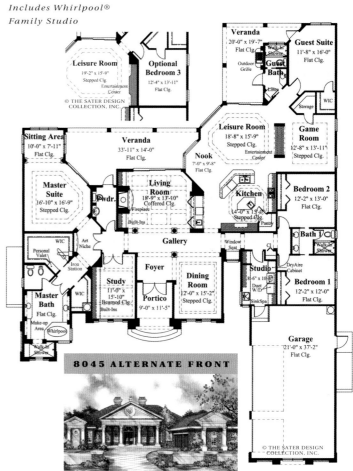

8041 ALTERNATE FRONT

VISIT OUR WEBSITE FOR MORE INFORMATION

8045 ALTERNATE FRONT

VISIT OUR WEBSITE FOR MORE INFORMATION

Gullane

St. Germain

Plan 8031a

5 Bed / 5-1/2 Bath

Living Area: 4,475 sq ft

Width: 58'0" / Depth: 65'0"

Exterior Walls: 2x6

Foundation:
Slab or Optional Basement

Price Code: **L2**

1st Floor: 2,164 sq ft

2nd Floor: 2,311 sq ft

Includes Whirlpool® Family Studio

REAR ELEVATION

© THE SATER DESIGN COLLECTION, INC.

Plan 8026

5 Bed / 5-1/2 Bath

Living Area: 4,167 sq ft

Width: 58'0" / Depth: 65'0"

Exterior Walls: 2x6

Foundation:
Slab or Optional Basement

Price Code: **L2**

REAR ELEVATION

© THE SATER DESIGN COLLECTION, INC.

1st Floor: 1,996 sq ft

2nd Floor: 2,171 sq ft

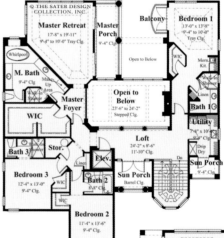

Garnett

Solaine

Plan 8047

5 Bed / 4-1/2 Bath

Living Area: 4,151 sq ft

Width: 80'0" / Depth: 96'6"

Exterior Walls: 2x6

Foundation: Slab

Price Code: **L2**

REAR ELEVATION

© THE SATER DESIGN COLLECTION, INC.

1st Floor: 2,852 sq ft

2nd Floor: 969 sq ft

Guest Suite: 330 sq ft

Plan 8051

5 Bed / 3-1/2 Bath

Living Area: 3,578 sq ft

Width: 71'0" / Depth: 72'0"

Exterior Walls: 2x6

Foundation: Slab

Price Code: **L1**

REAR ELEVATION

© THE SATER DESIGN COLLECTION, INC.

1st Floor: 2,163 sq ft

2nd Floor: 1,415 sq ft

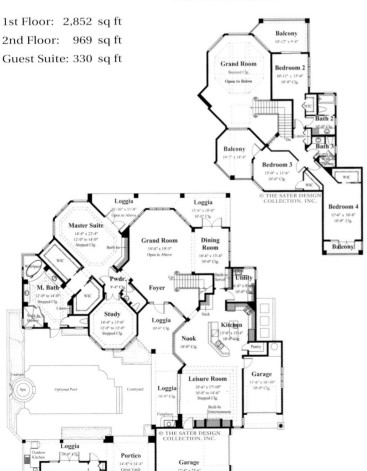

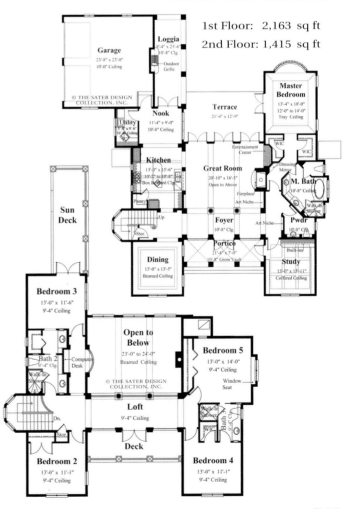

Christabel

Argentellas

Plan 8053a/*8052

4 Bed / 3-1/2 Bath

Living Area: 3,271 sq ft

Width: 74'8" / Depth: 118'0"

Exterior Walls: 2x6

Foundation: Slab

Price Code: **C4**

1st Floor: 2,974 sq ft

Guest Suite: 297 sq ft

Includes Whirlpool® Family Studio

REAR ELEVATION

© THE SATER DESIGN COLLECTION, INC.

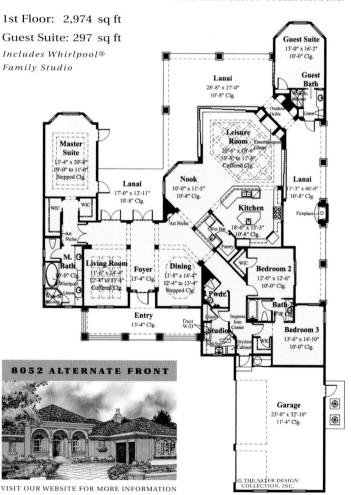

8052 ALTERNATE FRONT

VISIT OUR WEBSITE FOR MORE INFORMATION

Plan 8056

5 Bed / 4-1/2 Bath

Living Area: 4,398 sq ft

Width: 69'4" / Depth: 95'4"

Exterior Walls: 2x6

Foundation:
Slab or Optional Basement

Price Code: **L2**

1st Floor: 2,920 sq ft

2nd Floor: 1,478 sq ft

REAR ELEVATION

© THE SATER DESIGN COLLECTION, INC.

Plan 8060/*8058

4 Bed / 3-1/2 Bath

Living Area: 3,166 sq ft

Width: 67'0" / Depth: 91'8"

Exterior Walls: 2x6 or 8" CBS

Foundation: Slab

Price Code: **C4**

REAR ELEVATION

© THE SATER DESIGN COLLECTION, INC.

Plan 8064

4 Bed / 3-1/2 Bath

Living Area: 4,875 sq ft

Width: 95'0" / Depth: 82'8"

Exterior Walls: 2x6

Foundation:

Slab or Optional Basement

Price Code: **L2**

REAR ELEVATION

© THE SATER DESIGN COLLECTION, INC.

1st Floor: 3,588 sq ft

2nd Floor: 1,287 sq ft

8058 ALTERNATE FRONT

VISIT OUR WEBSITE FOR MORE INFORMATION

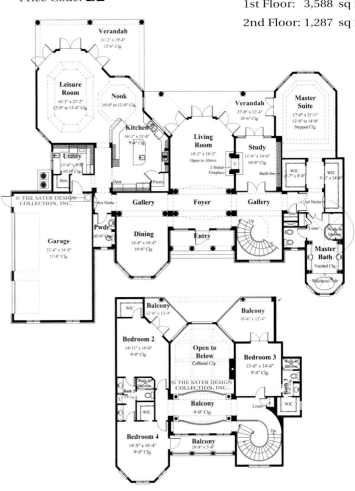

Luxury Index

TO ORDER, SEE
PAGES 254 & 255

PLAN NAME	PLAN #	PRICE CODE	PAGE	SQ. FT.
Monticello	6907	PSE5	112	4,255
Vintage Trace Way	6637	L2	178	4,187
St. Germain	8026	L2	244	4,167
Garnett	8047	L2	245	4,151
Stoney Creek Way	6656a	L2	233	4,140
Anna Belle	6782	L2	236	4,091
Monterray Lane	6672a	PSE5	56	4,009
La Riviere	8011	L2	237	3,988
Stoney Creek Lane	6649	L1	239	3,980
Royal Country Down	8001a	L1	236	3,977
Reynolds Plantation*	6722	L1	228	3,958
Winthrop	8034	PSE5	124	3,954
Cypress Point Court	6639	L1	176	3,944
Broadmoor Walk	6641a	L1	146	3,896
Fiddler's Creek	6746a	L1	228	3,893
The Cardiff	6750a	PSE5	192	3,883
Griffith Parkway	6721	L1	228	3,872
Castlepines Trace	6640	L1	198	3,866
Esmerelda Court	6737	PSE5	98	3,825
Beauchamp	8044a	L1	243	3,790
Demetri*	8045	L1	243	3,764
Cotton Creek Trace	6650	L1	233	3,748
Sunningdale Cove	6660a	L2	142	3,744
Old Marsh Circle	6642	L1	182	3,743
Bay Landing Drive	6676	L1	231	3,714
Coral Harbor	6728	L1	227	3,696
Rosewood Court	6733a	PSE5	132	3,688
Jasper Park	6941	PSE5	208	3,674
Waterford Place	6647	L1	232	3,670
Aubrey	8016	L1	242	3,611
Bellamy	8018	L1	242	3,610
Whispering Pines	6736	L1	230	3,599
Edgewood Court	6646	L1	239	3,588

*See our website www.luxuryplans.com for more plan information.

**MEDITERRANEAN
LUXURY HOME PLAN BOOK**

DAN SATER'S MEDITERRANEAN HOME PLANS

65 Mediterranean-style floor plans

In this unmatched portfolio of more than 65 unique home plans you will experience Mediterranean design in a new realm — one that delights, challenges and encourages the imagination. Superb architectural detail infuse sun-baked courtyards and loggias, while open floor plans stretch the boundaries of traditional Mediterranean style.

2,700 to over 8,000 sq ft

$14.95 *192 full-color pages*

**COTTAGES & VILLAS
COASTAL HOME PLAN BOOK**

DAN SATER'S COTTAGES & VILLAS

80 elegant cottage and waterfront home plans

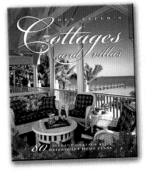

A photo tour of 8 stunning coastal homes previews a portfolio of eighty beautifully rendered charming clapboard cottages and grand Mediterranean villas. These highly versatile designs balance function with style and bring to mind a relaxed attitude.

1,200 — 4,300 sq ft

$14.95 *224 full-color pages*

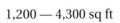

EUROPEAN LUXURY HOME PLANS

65 elevations and floor plans

Italian, French, English and Spanish styles. Here are sixty-five truly innovative plans inspired by history-rich European styles as diverse as America's own culture. These coastal villas, romantic chateaux and rambling retreats reinterpret the past to create a new breed of authentic design, rich with links to the outdoors. With a host of amenities, such as courtyards, porticos, disappearing walls and richly detailed interiors, these designs are sure to be classics.

2,200 — 4,600 sq ft

$12.95 *160 full-color pages*

**EUROPEAN
LUXURY HOME PLAN BOOK**

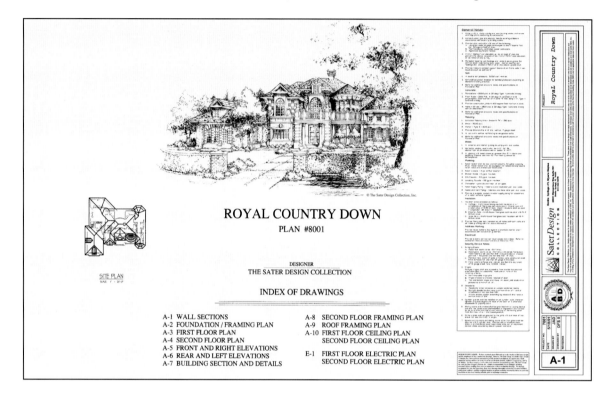

A-1 COVER SHEET/INDEX & SITE PLAN

An Artist's Rendering of the exterior of the house shows you approximately how the house will look when built and landscaped. The Index is a list of the sheets included and page numbers for easy reference. The Site Plan is a scaled drawing of the house to help determine the placement of the home on a building site.

A-2 WALL SECTION / NOTES

This sheet shows details of the house from the roof to the foundation. This section specifies the home's construction, insulation, flooring and roofing details.

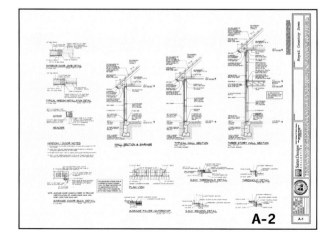

A-3 FOUNDATION PLAN

This sheet gives the foundation layout, including support walls, excavated and unexcavated areas, if any, and foundation notes. If the foundation is monolithic slab rather than basement, the plan shows footing and details.

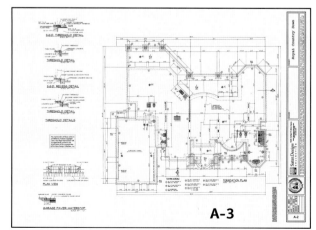

A-4 DETAILED FLOOR PLANS

These plans show the layout of each floor of the house. Rooms and interior spaces are carefully dimensioned and keys are given for cross-section details provided later in the plans, as well as window and door size callouts. These plans also show the location of kitchen appliances and bathroom fixtures, etc.

A-5 CEILING PLAN

Sater ceiling treatments are typically very detailed. This plan shows ceiling layout and extensive details.

A-6 ROOF PLAN

Overall layout and necessary details for roof construction are provided. If trusses are used, we suggest using a local truss manufacturer to design your trusses to comply with your local codes and regulations.

A-7 EXTERIOR ELEVATIONS

Included are front, rear, left and right sides of the house. Exterior materials, details and measurements are also given.

A-8 CROSS SECTION & DETAILS

Important changes in floor, ceiling and roof heights or the relationship of one level to another are called out. Also shown, when applicable, are exterior details such as railing and banding.

A-9 INTERIOR ELEVATIONS

These plans show the specific details and design of cabinets, utility rooms, fireplaces, bookcases, built-in units and other special interior features, depending on the nature and complexity of the item.

A-10 SECOND FLOOR FRAMING

This sheet shows directional spacing for floor trusses, beam locations and load-bearing conditions, if any.

E-1 ELECTRICAL PLAN

This sheet shows wiring and the suggested locations for switches, fixtures and outlets.

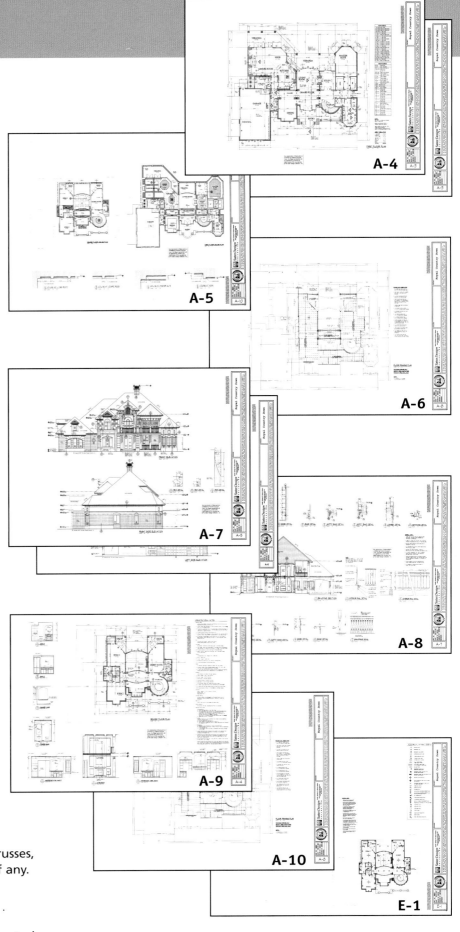

QUICK TURNAROUND

Because you are placing your order directly, we can ship plans to you quickly. If your order is placed before noon EST, we can usually have your plans to you the next business day. Some restrictions may apply. We cannot ship to a post office box; please provide a physical street address.

OUR EXCHANGE POLICY

Since our blueprints are printed especially for you at the time you place your order, we cannot accept any returns. If, for some reason, you find that the plan that you purchased does not meet your needs, then you may exchange that plan for another plan in our collection. We allow you sixty days from the time of purchase to make an exchange. At the time of the exchange, you will be charged a processing fee of 20% of the total amount of the original order, plus the difference in price between the plans (if applicable) and the cost to ship the new plans to you. Vellums cannot be exchanged. All sets must be approved and authorization given before the exchange can take place. Please call our customer service department if you have any questions.

LOCAL BUILDING CODES AND ZONING REQUIREMENTS

Our plans are designed to meet or exceed national building standards. Because of the great differences in geography and climate, each state, county and municipality has its own building codes and zoning requirements. Your plan may need to be modified to comply with local requirements regarding snow loads, energy codes, soil and seismic conditions and a wide range of other matters. Prior to using plans ordered from us, we strongly advise that you consult a local building official.

ARCHITECTURE AND ENGINEERING SEALS

Some cities and states are now requiring that a licensed architect or engineer review and approve any set of building documents prior to construction. This is due to concerns over energy costs, safety, structural integrity and other factors. Prior to applying for a building permit or the start of actual construction, we strongly advise that you consult your local building official who can tell you if such a review is required.

DISCLAIMER

We have put substantial care and effort into the creation of our blueprints. We authorize the use of our blueprints on the express condition that you strictly comply with all local building codes, zoning requirements and other applicable laws, regulations and ordinances. However, because we cannot provide on-site consultation, supervision or control over actual construction, and because of the great variance in local building requirements, building practices and soil, seismic, weather and other conditions, WE CANNOT MAKE ANY WARRANTY, EXPRESS OR IMPLIED, WITH RESPECT TO THE CONTENT OR USE OF OUR BLUEPRINTS OR VELLUMS, INCLUDING BUT NOT LIMITED TO ANY WARRANTY OF MERCHANTABILITY OR OF FITNESS FOR A PARTICULAR PURPOSE. Please Note: Floor plans in this book are not construction documents and are subject to change. Renderings are artist's concept only.

HOW MANY SETS OF PRINTS WILL YOU NEED?

We offer a single set of prints so that you can study and plan your dream home in detail. However, you cannot build from this package. One set of blueprints is marked "NOT FOR CONSTRUCTION." If you are planning to obtain estimates from a contractor or subcontractor, or if you are planning to build immediately, you will need more sets. Because additional sets are less expensive, make sure you order enough to satisfy all your requirements. Sometimes changes are needed to a plan; in that case, we offer vellums that are reproducible and erasable so changes can be made directly to the plans. Vellums are the only set that can be reproduced; it is illegal to copy blueprints. The checklist below will help you determine how many sets are needed.

Plan checklist

_____ **Owner** (one for notes, one for file)

_____ **Builder** (generally requires at least three sets; one as a legal document, one for inspections and at least one to give subcontractors)

_____ **Local Building Department** (often requires two sets)

_____ **Mortgage Lender** (usually one set for a conventional loan; three sets for FHA or VA loans)

_____ **Total Number of Sets**

IGNORING COPYRIGHT LAWS CAN BE A
$1,000,000 mistake!

Recent changes in the US copyright laws allow for statutory penalties of up to $150,000 per incident for copyright infringement involving any of the copyrighted plans found in this publication. The law can be confusing. So, for your own protection, take the time to understand what you cannot do when it comes to home plans.

WHAT YOU CAN'T DO!
YOU CANNOT DUPLICATE HOME PLANS
YOU CANNOT COPY ANY PART OF A HOME PLAN TO CREATE ANOTHER
YOU CANNOT BUILD A HOME WITHOUT BUYING A BLUEPRINT OR LICENSE

How to order plans | BY PHONE, BY MAIL OR ON-LINE

SATER DESIGN COLLECTION, INC.
25241 Elementary Way, Suite 201
Bonita Springs, FL 34135
1-800-718-7526

www.saterdesign.com
sales@saterdesign.com

ADDITIONAL ITEMS

11x17 Color Rendering Front Perspective* $100.00
Materials List* $75.00
Additional Blueprints (per set) $65.00
Reverse Mirror-Image Blueprints $50.00
*Call for availability. Special orders may require additional fees.

POSTAGE AND HANDLING

Overnight $52.00
2nd Day $42.00
Ground $32.00
Saturday $72.00
For shipping international, please call for a quote.

BLUEPRINT PRICE SCHEDULE*

	5 SETS	8 SETS	VELLUM
C1	$725	$785	$970
C2	$770	$830	$1040
C3	$820	$890	$1120
C4	$875	$940	$1200
L1	$1015	$1100	$1365
L2	$1090	$1185	$1490
L3	$1210	$1300	$1655
L4	$1325	$1420	$1820
PSE5	Call for pricing		

* Prices subject to change without notice

Order form

PLAN NUMBER _____

Check one: ☐ Visa ☐ MasterCard

Credit Card Number _____

Expiration Date _____

Signature _____

☐ 5-set building package . . . . $_____
☐ 8-set building package . . . . $_____
☐ 1-set of reproducible vellums . . . . $_____

____ Additional Identical Blueprints @ $65 each $_____
____ Reverse Mirror-Image Blueprints @ $50 fee $_____

Sub-Total $_____
Shipping and Handling $_____
Sales Tax (FL Res.) 6% $_____

TOTAL $_____

Name _____

Company _____

Street _____

City _____ State_____ Zip_____

Daytime Telephone Number (_____)_____

Check one:

☐ Consumer   ☐ Builder   ☐ Developer

Special Thanks

We'd like to extend our gratitude to those who have
helped make this book possible.

BUILDERS:

Cronacher Homes

DeAngelis Diamond

Enterprise Construction

Harbourside Custom Homes

Heritage Homes

Hunt Construction

Jeff Leitch

Lifestyle Concepts

London Bay Homes

Slocum-Christian

Snell Construction

Wyman Stokes Builder

INTERIOR DESIGNERS:

Freestyle Design Studio

Jett & Company

Marc-Michaels

Vince Muller

PHOTOGRAPHERS:

Everett & Soulé • Tom Harper

Dan Forer • Joseph Lapeyra

Michael Lowry • William Minarich

Kim Sargent • Bruce Schaeffer

Laurence Taylor • Doug Thompson

Oscar Thompson • CJ Walker